ANTHEM

Stories of True Transformation in Portland, Oregon

Published in Beaverton, Oregon, by Good Catch Publishing.
www.goodcatchpublishing.com
V1.1

Printed in the United States of America

Table of Contents

DEDICATION

This book is dedicated to those who have ever wondered if the life they are living is really all there is. This is for those who secretly wish for something more.

If the story of your life is tragically less than you had hoped, if your past continues to limit your attempts at a better future or if you feel like you are trapped in the consequences of poor choices, then this book is for you.

This is for all those who want the story of their life, no matter the beginning, to be transformed into an anthem of hope, strength and true inspiration. Your story can begin a new chapter today!

ACKNOWLEDGEMENTS

I would like to thank Bob and Jenny Donnelly, as well as Brad Makowski, for their vision for this book and Hannah Partridge for her hard work in making it a reality. And to the people of Anthem, thank you for your boldness and vulnerability in sharing your personal stories.

This book would not have been published without the amazing efforts of our project manager and editor, Hayley Pandolph. Her untiring resolve pushed this project forward and turned it into a stunning victory. Thank you for your great fortitude and diligence. Deep thanks to our incredible Editor in Chief, Michelle Cuthrell, and Executive Editor, Jen Genovesi, for all the amazing work they do. I would also like to thank our invaluable proofreader, Melody Davis, for the focus and energy she has put into perfecting our words.

Lastly, I want to extend our gratitude to the creative and very talented Jenny Randle, who designed the beautiful cover for *Anthem: Stories of True Transformation in Portland, Oregon.*

Daren Lindley
President and CEO
Good Catch Publishing

The book you are about to read
is a compilation of authentic life stories.
The facts are true, and the events are real.
These storytellers have dealt with crisis, tragedy, abuse
and neglect and have shared their most private moments,
mess-ups and hang-ups in order for others to learn and
grow from them. In order to protect the identities of those
involved in their pasts, the names and details of some
storytellers have been withheld or changed.

INTRODUCTION

The book in your hands has the potential to be the inspiration and encouragement you have been looking for. A quick look at our world today causes great concern and stirs a myriad of questions about the future. Shootings in malls, schools and hospitals — places that we used to consider safe — are now potential places of danger. People everywhere are wondering if our society is slipping further into danger and darkness. But life in the darkness is not a new thing. People all around us live lives of quiet desperation. It's likely that you or someone you know is living in a desperate, dark world right now. Perhaps it's a hidden addiction or a debilitating shame from a history of poor choices. Maybe your relationships are a long trail of heartaches, and your biggest fear is that your future promises only more of the same. The truth is you are not alone. The great question that is begging for an answer and what everyone really wants to know is simply this: Is it possible to have authentic hope for a better tomorrow? Can a life really change? Can habits and recurring failure be transformed into success and peace? The answer is yes! Miracles do happen!

These are the stories of seven people who live right here in the Portland area. They are living proof that the past does not have the final say. Their stories are ones of difficulty, addiction, poor decisions and despair that have been transformed into an anthem of success, freedom and happiness. Their stories are inspiring, filled with hope, authentic and heart-moving. As you read their own accounts and journey with them through the shadow of their yesterdays, you will come to know the secret of their breakthroughs. You'll see the simple truths that anyone, no matter the circumstances, can take advantage of to see his or her world transformed. The song of your life can truly become a song of celebration — a great anthem of victory, purpose and fulfillment as you read through the pages of this book. Enjoy!

LONER ON THE HEIGHTS
The Story of Michael McGinn
Written by Richard Drebert

My helmet beam cast eerie shadows along the iron ceiling of the oil tanker's empty belly. I slipped a steel hook through the rat hole (eyelet) in a metal beam a couple feet above my head and hung from my two foot stirrups for an instant. I rope-walked a long step in midair, swinging my tense body beneath the beams — 130 feet above the vessel's deck. At the center of my back, I felt the satisfying tension in my retractable lifeline.

Riggers stared up at me as I swung and clung like a spider between lofty girders that resembled the ribcage of a dead whale. Each rat hole in a rib received my steel safety hook and was attached to the top end of my rope stirrup. I dangled from these stirrups and swung in them from rib to rib, spaced about 4 feet apart. In my wake, I fastened straps and pulleys into each vacated rat hole from which riggers would suspend vertical steel cables. Struts (steel braces) between these cables would support tiers of planks as scaffolding.

In this massive steel canyon, welders' voices echoed far below as they waited for me to descend on a safety line after anchoring the last pulley on a beam.

I knew of two rope walkers working inside tankers

who fell to their deaths — our protective systems weren't perfect, and sometimes we ignored safety mandates. Often we rope walkers free-climbed when our lifelines tangled — or if it wasn't *comfortable.*

But clinging to ropes at devilish heights never chilled me — or my father, who worked as an emergency lineman for Pacific Power and Light. That *fear of falling* gene had skipped us both.

And it wasn't a plunge off a high-voltage tower that killed my father — and set me on a reckless path free-climbing my way through life …

కాకాకా

As a boy, I never worried when Dad rushed to the airport on emergency calls. He worked with the PP&L emergency response team that flew all over the Pacific Northwest, restoring electricity to shivering families after storms knocked out the power grids. I believed he was invincible.

Dad loved the Game of Kings and seldom missed his weekend pilgrimage to the golf course near our home. My 6-foot, 3-inch Irish giant and I strode like monarch and prince onto the beautiful green together — when only hours before, Dad had been handling 700,000-volt transmission lines in high winds and soaking rain.

My father had grown up a loner, nearly raising himself after divorce broke up his parents. Bitterness bled through his personality when we visited my grandma, Naida, and his stepdad, Pete, in Vancouver. Grandma bought a house with a den reserved for Dad when our family visited on holidays. He shunned visits to Naida and Pete unless he had a place to escape. Dad lounged in his den with the television, while everyone else chattered elsewhere.

Mom had a difficult childhood, too, but Dad loved Grandma Dottie and Mom's father, Grandpa Bruno — hardworking, hard-drinking Italians. We saw them often when I was young.

My father was an only child, but not me. My older sister, Ginger, was my babysitter and friend when Mom and Dad were away. We grew up in a tiny green house in North Portland, and after nearly 13 years, we knew every quirky neighbor on Central Street.

"Bye, Mom! I'm goin'!"

I bounded down the steps, waving my little Bible at Mr. Coffman, my church chauffeur, who unfolded himself from behind the steering wheel of a big black Lincoln Continental. Mr. Coffman leaned lanky arms on the roof of his car, smiling as I hopped in with other kids sardined in the backseat.

Mr. Coffman always wore a spotless black suit, no matter the weather, and he carried himself like a hulking funeral director.

"The church van's broke down again, kids …"

I didn't mind. My kind undertaker always delivered me to Sunday school at the Wesleyan Lutheran Chapel right on time. It was the gracious, caring people at my church who planted a single seed of truth in my soul, even though Dad's indifference to God confused me.

"If God's real, he's real; if he's not, he's not, Mike."

My parents had little time for religion — as long as there was work to do, beer in the fridge and a golf green nearby, Dad was happy; Mom had her friends and us kids to keep her busy. For the first 13 years of my life, my parents worked hand in glove, slapping the McGinn label on a bright future.

In 1980, Dad bought Mom her dream home, and the basement alone was nearly as big as our whole house on Central Street. The beautiful Northgate Park sprawled out our picture window, and we had two bathrooms instead of one frantic one. I left my boyhood chums in a different district and stayed to myself at my scary new Portsmouth Middle School. I was the only Irish-Italian oddball in my classes, and my best friend on my new street was a German Shepherd, who lived next door.

My father primed me to play football by challenging me with nickel bets on favorite NFL teams. I grew up studying every move of pigskin heroes; it seemed natural to put my own big hands and feet to work on a gridiron. Northgate Park had a football field right across the street, so I joined a Pop Warner Football team.

In my helmet and pads none of the older kids from my Portsmouth Middle School recognized me — but they *felt* me as I bashed my shoulders into their knees or intercepted their passes. Kids from Portsmouth admired the mystery kid in jersey 75. He seldom said a word after games or practices and trotted off the Northgate field to his house across the street.

Everything changed the morning I decided to wear a Pop Warner t-shirt with my number 75 to school.

"Whoa! *You* be number 75? Hey, it's the *ghost* who hits so hard!"

I basked in my newfound jock celebrity.

Leaving my old school, my friends, even my church behind didn't seem so bad after all. For a few months, my family nested in comfortable dreams — until my father moved away and never came back.

ବ୍ୟବ୍ୟବ୍ୟ

"How's Dad?"

It was my first question to Mom every evening as she fixed dinner after rushing home from the Portland hospital. Mom was a solemn, weary woman now, after watching my father endure his painful chemotherapy treatments.

When his lung cancer went into remission, I hoped that my bulletproof father had busted through the line, heading for a touchdown — but he faltered before reaching his goal. His cancer metastasized. Ginger and I were devastated when Mom told us that Dad had bone cancer, and there was no cure.

Dad's desertion from our day-to-day lives overwhelmed all of us. I missed his booming voice at 5:30

a.m. on Saturday morning: "Hey, Mike! Wanna go play a few rounds?"

Dad believed he was protecting his children from the trauma of watching him waste away, but Ginger and I only felt rejected and confused. The last time I visited him in his hospital room, Dad put on a brave face, but I barely recognized this frail man whom I loved so dearly.

I saw my dad alive only three times in his last seven months, and this season of grief ruined my tomorrows. One day my mentor was gone for good, and Ginger and I knew we were on our own. My big sister and I grew apart, retreating to safe places inside ourselves, where no one could "get to us."

Mom adjusted to a hard life as a single mother, tending bar late into the evenings. Often I remember the front door opening about 3 a.m. and turning over to go back to sleep. Like my father when he was a boy, I learned to fend for myself, living alone much of my teen years.

Less than a year after my father died, Mom faced foreclosure on her dream home, and her Italian hackles rose over the bank's ruthless ways of dealing.

"I'll burn it down before we give our house back!"

To avoid the looming financial ruin, she sold the house with all its bittersweet memories. We moved to a small rental on the other side of Northgate Park.

"Let me the h*** OUT!"

But no one in his right mind was going to unbolt the door to a classroom where a maniac fumed and screamed.

I was tossing student chairs at the door. After ripping off the chalkboards from the wall, I grabbed a desk and shattered a window — then Mom came.

She was mad, too — that they locked me in a classroom at all. But I was out of control. I simmered down when I knew she was outside, but as soon as the principal opened the door, I was *gone.* I needed a drink or a joint, and I headed off the middle school campus to find friends.

No one could read Mike McGinn, and I liked it that way. The rage inside me never left me, and after Dad died, I felt like I'd swallowed a cinderblock — it lodged in my guts. My only relief seemed to be when I beat on someone or some *thing*, or drank myself into a stupor, or got high.

At school, teachers were my enemies, and I didn't care if the whole world knew that I smoked pot or drank — they could *all* go to h***! Bring on the consequences, because pain distracted me from the constant throbbing anguish inside me.

My friends knew that a landmine might explode any second if they stood close to me. A boyhood chum made the mistake of saying something about my dad, and I threw him through the Portsmouth principal's window. Suspensions only fueled my hatred for school, and by the time Mom enrolled me at Roosevelt High, I attended classes only if I felt like it.

My junior year, my last year at school, I wandered the halls in search of friends so we could go party at someone's house. I was a man-sized kid, with a full mustache and beard, and I hung out with the druggies and drinkers at Roosevelt, who also hated school.

I had been driving since I was 14, never bothering to get a driver's license, and only once did I face a judge for a serious driving incident. One day I sideswiped a parked car in Mom's Mustang and sped away, leaving the scene of the accident.

No one came after me until Ginger drove through the same neighborhood a few days later. Someone recognized Mom's Mustang and its glaring dents that fit the gouges in his own vehicle like a jigsaw puzzle.

The authorities slapped my wrist for the hit-and-run and revoked my ability to obtain a driver's license until I was 18. But I didn't need a license, anyway. I believed that consequences were usually brief and painful and just part of my life.

Mom purchased a small home across the street from Roosevelt High, and I couldn't wait to move out on my own. I found a rental and a roommate, and we partied whenever I wasn't working. Stocking gut trucks wasn't my idea of fun, but I kept the warehouse job with Canteen Food Services for a couple of years. Canteen supplied chips, candy, etc., to workers all over the Portland waterfront, so with my connections, I found a better job.

On Swan Island, at the Portland docks, I landed employment as an apprentice welder, descending daily into the bowels of the cruise liners and freighters to repair tanks or boilers. It was a perfect place for me to hide from the world when I wasn't drinking at my favorite bar or smoking pot with other addicts. The more hours of back-breaking work the better, and I believed that I was living up to my father's hard-driving McGinn legacy.

Yet if my dad ever felt fulfillment in restoring heat and lights to the homes of little old ladies and schools, his brand of satisfaction eluded me completely. Sometimes I wondered if starting a family (as he had) might dislodge the relentless heaviness in my soul. But how could a woman ever fit into my lifestyle — patching up ships by day and drinking and smoking weed late into the night?

During my years as a welder, I never seriously contemplated adding a steady relationship to my life until the night I met Denise. She was my life-altering blind date, which I expected to be a bust. Instead, the woman fascinated me. Over several beers and games of darts, I found out that she had a 4-year-old son named Daniel and that she wasn't looking for a long-term relationship, either.

But as the bar emptied and her friends grew restless to leave, I was changing my mind. In Denise's blue eyes I discovered an intense invitation that came from someone other than this beautiful woman. A feeling stole through my intoxicated mind that through Denise I might find true peace.

On our dates, Denise broached the subject of religion sometimes, but only a sliver of light slipped through my selfish fog at the time. Although she had been struggling in her life, she had clung to her belief in a Jesus who had been her friend since she was a little girl. Denise believed that God cared for her more than any man ever could.

I wasn't put off by Denise's religion talk. In fact, our conversations about the Bible intrigued me. I was bowled over by her depth of character, and I welded shut the door of my heart with this wonderful woman inside.

After a few months, I convinced her that I was raw material for a lasting relationship. We moved in together, and suddenly I was a father.

෯෯෯

It felt right, like my dad must have felt when he and Mom married — but I didn't see a need for a marriage certificate to seal the deal. I went to work as a rope walker, and the danger-filled high work sometimes took me out of the country to the Orient for weeks at a time. I often worked 12-hour days, seven days a week, and Denise tolerated my strange lifestyle. The money was good, and I began to raise Daniel the way Dad raised me.

We had our second child, Charissa, and with more responsibilities I stepped up my drinking and smoking pot. Denise hated it and hid her fears, praying that I would quit, but I was willingly blind to her concerns. Unlike arc eye (temporary impairment from staring into the bright ultraviolet welder's flame), my blindness to the gift of my family was growing *permanent*. This beautiful woman's unconditional love reminded me of how wretched I was.

One day I lost my temper and threw away my high-paying rope-walking job. Our ramrod was simply living up to his name. "Seagull" would show up at a jobsite, crap all over everyone and fly away. I was at the end of my rope. I was in Los Angeles at the time, and I called Denise when Seagull canceled my Portland airplane ticket — out of spite.

"It's for the best, Mike. I'll wire you the money. Come on home."

Denise still stayed with me, even though my addictive behavior was growing too much for our family to bear.

❧❧❧

One day out of the blue, when unemployment checks were about to run out, an old friend from Pop Warner Football days knocked on the door.

"Mike, you lookin' for a job?"

"D*** right."

"Ever carry hod? It's hard work, but good pay. You'd be all over the state."

Perfect.

I jumped at the chance — without a clue that this age-old trade would ultimately reroute my future.

A hod (mortar) carrier knows what it means to be under the gun in burning heat or knuckle-numbing cold. The hoddy is responsible for mixing mortar for block layers and delivering the hod, minute by minute, to the masons troweling mortar to stabilize block or brick. The hoddy is the first to prep a job, by setting up scaffolding, and the last to leave a job, tearing it all down.

It was at the end of this season working with block masons that I slipped closer to a point of no return. At every break between muscling mud, I drank beer or smoked pot. At lunchtime, too. Then after work, my friends and I hit the local bars or tailgated a few six-packs.

At home, an uncomfortable feeling nibbled at my conscience when I passed Denise's open Bible on the coffee table. I thought that I was pretty broadminded, tolerating her religion talk. I saw myself as my wife's family provider — a man's man who didn't give a d*** what anyone thought of him, including the faithful woman who loved him.

As I strayed, Denise grew more dependent upon this Jesus she talked about and less dependent upon me. She sensed that I was headed for disaster, and if she stayed with me, she would see her children and herself mangled at the bottom with me.

It wasn't long after I had purchased Denise a new house that I came home one day to find her gone: kids, clothing, car seat, knick-knacks. Even the fragrance of her perfume had left the premises. I popped a top and flopped into a chair where the stench of beer reminded me of the years I had lived alone. I hated remembering … I hated *me* — but I could face any consequences. It was my lot in life. A razor-sharp sense of rejection cut through me as I pictured my father's face.

Dad didn't even want to see me before he died …

My feeling of abandonment hit me hard, and I picked up the phone.

My drinking buddy answered. "Hey, man. I'm on one — let's party." My throat felt raw, and I hoped alcohol would deaden the feelings of loss. I told myself that I didn't care, beating back emotions that threatened to overwhelm me. I loved Denise. I loved my kids. How could I live without them?

Suddenly my adolescent rage rescued me from guilt, and I spun rubber to a secluded place to get stoned. By the time I stumbled into our dream home the next morning, I had racked up a DUI — the first one I ever had. While booking me, the police ferreted out my sordid driving record, which screamed SCOFFLAW! (At 18 years old, my license had been suspended — and it still was, more than 10 years later.)

In the following weeks, I smoked pot incessantly and drank all night, after slinging mud and setting up scaffolding for masonry jobs all day. Denise and I talked sometimes, mostly arguing over my lifestyle, but she wasn't budging. She said I had to quit *all* of it before she and the kids would come back.

I landed in jail again on my second DUI exactly 30 days after my first. My court dates were piling up, and I didn't give a d***.

No woman was going to tell me how to run my life. Our problems were her fault. I could go it alone.

Then I lost my job.

❧❧❧

When a great friend introduced me to a seductress in pure white, I fell hard.

I had never felt so enhanced, so alive. It was as if I had been asleep my whole life, and now I was awake. Suddenly I didn't care about looking for work, or my unemployment checks, or if I paid my bills. Sure, I had lost the house to foreclosure, but I melted any icy sense of failure by staying high.

When methamphetamine hit my brain, I smashed open the gates of perdition and stood up to the devil himself. I could take on anyone. I could work harder, drink harder and out-think everyone around me.

Where the h*** did all this extra time come from, anyway? For months I slept in tiny snippets between days and nights of partying. My new friends dominated every moment of my life, involving me in their projects, and I ate up their acceptance like a needy teenager. After all, they poisoned me for free. I never lacked for a line of meth whenever I wanted it.

Denise watched me leave my stirrups and freefall past her, and it broke her heart that I didn't even try to grab a rope as I plummeted down.

She was shocked every time I visited the kids. I was sucked up, lost to the outside world, eaten by a cancer of the soul, wasting away. My body twitched, and I had dropped 25 pounds, reflected in my bony shoulders and skeletal jaw line.

After nearly two years of being separated from Denise, I had moved into a nice apartment with a yard, and in sober moments I yearned to have my family back. Yet I demanded that our reconciling be on my dysfunctional terms.

Denise was praying. Not just to have her family healed — but for God to rescue me before I splattered against the iron deck rushing toward me. It must have been her petitions that slapped my conscience alive one morning.

One day I stood in my kitchen, suddenly sober, undone, realizing that the crack house I lived in was like me. At first, it was well-kept, solid, admired. Now everyone knew it was falling to pieces. Junkies had piled garbage on either side of the front door. Old cars on jack stands replaced lawn ornaments. Friends used a camper in the driveway to vomit in, then flop inside to sleep off binges. My home was ruined.

I threw a few things in a knapsack and walked away from the meth, the friends, the house — not to rehab, but to my mother's home across from Roosevelt High. I wanted my family back, and I had to start over before I hit the cold iron deck and died.

Twenty years ago, in my childish egotism, I would have bragged that the McGinn grit helped me kick my meth addiction. I would have told you that I had no mentors, no real friends to help me, so I grabbed hold of cable on the way to the bottom and *saved myself* — but I know better now.

A force far stronger than my own will protected me for pivotal moments of decision. The seed planted by kind people like my undertaker, and nurtured by Denise, had survived the drugs, the rage, the corruption in my life, and finally it began to take root.

It's the only way I can explain the miracle of my choice and ability to kill my addictions: to alcohol, to pot, to deadly methamphetamine.

But consequences are often retroactive in a man's life ...

In my two-year plummet toward annihilation, I had been arrested for receiving stolen property and did time in jail for other minor offenses. While living with my mom, my probation violations suddenly stacked up on a judge's desk, and he sent the police to track me down.

The authorities were like block layers, screaming at me to deliver more mud — and I couldn't keep up! It was just easier to ignore their warrants for my arrest as long as possible.

Denise saw that I was determined to stay clean and sober, and she and the kids moved into Mom's house with me. Then the sledgehammer came down: The cops showed up one afternoon and handcuffed Daddy in front of my whole family.

Standing before the judge in my orange jumpsuit, I told him dejectedly, "Your Honor, I'm tired of all the probations and violations and warrants — just give me jail time, and be done with it."

The judge obliged and slapped me with 18 months. With my time served, work time and good behavior, I spent six months in a room with 50 other druggies and thieves. Being warehoused at the Inverness Jail in Multnomah County convinced me that my lifestyle as a hard-charging free climber was over for good.

Denise rented an apartment in Gresham, still on pins and needles about what I would do when I hit the streets a free man.

"Mike, I love you. But if you go back to the way you used to be, don't bother coming home." It was her ultimatum that helped me lock the door on the past. I had to fundamentally change who I was as a man or lose *everything.* Was this even possible?

After taking public transportation to Gresham, I hoofed it along the streets, thinking of my new baby daughter, Hannah, and hoping for the fairytale reunion I had replayed in my mind for months. A peculiar incident rolled around in my head as I walked.

Brad, a hard case I knew on the streets, was sitting on his bunk at Inverness, reading the Bible, and I commented how surprised I was.

He said, "I read the Bible to give me peace of mind, Mike."

Had I ever known peace in my whole selfish existence?

I wasn't disappointed as I walked into Denise's living room, and I melted into her arms surrounded by my kids. Standing there, I set my jaw toward a sober family life — no job, no prospects, but full of hope.

༄ ༄ ༄

On probation again.

I would rather have slept in on Sunday mornings, but Denise wouldn't tolerate it. She had our church all picked out, and it was right across the street. I spent a few months as a millwright before starting permanent work as a hod carrier for a masonry outfit where a couple old friends worked. I knew it would take time for Denise to trust me again, and going to church (I sat in the pew expecting lightning to strike) was proof of my commitment to her and the kids. I didn't expect to really meet God there.

But Brad was right. When someone read the Bible, I really did feel peaceful. Maybe it was high time that I made a commitment to religion after all.

Denise's life had radically changed while we were muddling through the years together, and her relationship with Jesus was stronger than ever. At church I started to pray to God the way I was taught at our Lutheran church when I was a kid, and sometimes I really felt like he was listening.

A couple weeks before my daughter Charissa was scheduled to be baptized, Denise issued a very strong suggestion: "You need to get baptized, too, Mike."

It was the perfect way for me to bond with my wife and kids. It was a win-win — all I had to do was overcome my fear of standing in front of the whole church!

After Charissa and I were baptized, I felt different somehow. I stood high above the horizons of my past and realized that I had lived like a loner, but *never was alone*. I should have been dead and buried a dozen times, considering my reckless lifestyle, but someone, for some reason, had saved me.

And if Jesus truly was the one who saved me, I needed to learn about him at any cost.

I set out to try to understand the Bible, and Denise was amazed to see my metamorphosis begin: from a secretive, bound-up significant other, to a partner who showed his gratitude for her commitment. Now when she sent me off to work, she knew that I wasn't dumping my sandwiches and getting high for lunch.

One day, in Yakima, Washington, I was tasked to break down scaffolding, where I worked 20 feet above hard-packed gravel. Our block walls rested on concrete footings, and beneath me, pieces of rebar stabbed the air about 32 inches high.

It was a great view of the city from my high vantage. I was unhurriedly stacking wood planks, one on top of the other, when I uncharacteristically lost my balance. My toe caught the edge of the stack, and I stumbled forward, easily straddling the pile of planks with one boot. I should have recovered my balance like I always did — but my foot descended like I had stepped on a rotten stair.

My momentum carried me downward, and I knew that my full weight rested on a plank with no support beneath it — a widow maker. I plunged headfirst, a** over teakettle, my empty hardhat knocking about the steel uprights. My body never stopped until the top of my bare head hit the earth.

I lay for an instant, stunned, between rebar stubs. I knew that a forklift would soon careen around the corner to pick up more disassembled scaffolding — so, from my back, I waved my hands in the air. The driver skidded to a stop when he saw me on the ground.

"Mike! You okay?"

I wasn't. Blood oozed from the top of my head. I tried to sit up, but my head flopped onto my chest like a dead chicken's.

Lying on my back, I was wide awake, surprisingly feeling little discomfort, and I tested my legs and feet and toes. They all moved fine, so how bad could it be? Paramedics loaded me into an ambulance, and we screamed off to the hospital.

Denise didn't believe the nurse at the other end of the line when she told her that I had fallen from a scaffold. No way — it had to be a bad joke from some of Mike's old friends. Mike was a rope walker. He felt just as much at home 100 feet in the air as he did in his easy chair!

The nurse handed the phone to me. "No, she's got it right, hon. I fell on my head ... everything still seems to work ... I'll meet you at Portland Oregon Health and Science University. People here say they're better equipped to handle broken necks ..."

The brightly lit Intensive Care Unit at OHSU seemed as cold and unfriendly as the physician who poked and probed my neck and back. Finally, he shook his head.

"Look, Mr. McGinn, X-rays don't lie: The impact of your fall has damaged your C-2, C-6 and C-7 vertebrae."

It was time to tell the man one more time: "I can move my feet and legs and toes, too, Doc. And I never really felt much pain at all …"

"Mr. McGinn, I want you to know that you *should* be paralyzed or dead right now."

But I wasn't — either one.

"A broken C-2 alone put Christopher Reeve (the now-deceased Superman) in a wheelchair for life," he muttered and left me alone to chew on his diagnosis.

Denise stood by, praying, and I submitted to more exams by a few more doctors. They settled on a procedure to stabilize my upper body before surgery — a contraption known in medical parlance as a halo. They were about to start drilling holes in my head for screws, when a senior physician derailed their whole morbid plan.

"Let's try a neck brace instead, to keep him stationary — it might give the vertebrae a chance to heal themselves."

Thank God.

Denise was my rock during the whole uncomfortable bracing process. She prayed with me, encouraging me. Loving me. In my hospital room, over and over, physicians told me, "There's no reason you should *not* be dead."

The following day, I fell into my old ways of dealing with pain and uncertainty: I chided myself that I should buck up and *bear the consequences.* I didn't need anyone's pity or compassion.

But on my first day of total immobility, I began to feel *unhinged.*

If God is real, he's real. If he's not, he's not.

Dad's words rolled around in my head like mud in a mortar mixer, and I feared that I really was on my own in this world after all.

That second day after my fall, Denise stood by my bed, cheerful and compassionate like usual, with her faith in her Jesus set like concrete. She was my head nurse, always watching over me like a guardian angel, so when she checked over my wounded crown, it wasn't unusual.

"What's this, Mike?"

I thought, *Oh, no, what now?* She moved my hair around, frowning.

I could see her blue eyes beginning to tear up as she said, "Oh, *Lord*..." and I swallowed hard.

"Mike ..." Her words caught in her throat. "There's a handprint ... on your head."

"What do you mean, Dee Dee?"

"I see fingerprints, like they're burned down to the skin. Five of them — a perfect shape, as if your head was cradled by ... God's hand. It's easy to see, Michael!"

I remembered how Denise had cradled Hannah's little head; it was the picture of love and protection, and it shook me to the bone. Nothing on our jobsite remotely resembled these five fingers of God's delivering hand.

I just plain cried as I realized that Jesus must have absorbed my consequences.

The next time the physician examined me, he was glad he made the call to clamp me into a brace rather than screw on a halo. My C-2 vertebrae had begun to heal in a matter of days.

To be able to move my limbs with a broken neck defied logic and even science — but not *faith.* I finished out the week at the hospital and left for home, knowing that God held the blueprint of my life — not the doctors, and not me. God was turning my whole world upside down!

Denise delivered me to OHSU for spinal surgery, just two weeks after my two-story crash, and after a four-day stint in the hospital, I went home to heal, bolted in an upper body straightjacket. For weeks Denise had me all to herself — and she never let me forget that Jesus was the reason I was alive.

"Pay attention, Mike! Jesus is waiting for you to accept him as your Savior."

After weeks of immobility and six months of painful physical therapy, my masonry boss wanted me back at my old job. Incredibly, I was able to grab a wheelbarrow and shovel hod again.

Denise and I bought a home across town, and in time, I apprenticed as a block layer. Our church across the street from us in Gresham became God's gracious stepping stone for new beginnings.

We lived in a new community, and Denise launched out to find us a church close to home. A nephew recommended New Beginnings Christian Center, now called Anthem Church, and Dee Dee sensed God's touch there the first time she visited. She couldn't wait for me to experience it, too, and I followed her lead, knowing how Jesus spoke to our family through her.

Man, is this really *church*?

Pianos, guitars, drums ... the place rocked with Jesus-centered music, and I never spent a moment bored or wishing I was somewhere else.

At the close of a Sunday service, Pastor Brad did what he often does. He asked those in the sanctuary to close their eyes and lift a hand — to acknowledge that they needed a Savior.

I prayed for God to forgive me that day, and I gave Jesus my beat-up old *self* — body, mind and heart — once and for all.

Why had I waited so long?

The big coarse cinderblock that had rasped inside my soul for more than 30 years suddenly melted away like wax. Relief streamed into me, and God troweled his healing love into every nook and cranny of my heart, where guilt had once been.

Best of all, the constant dread of consequences disappeared, too. In its place, Jesus deposited the expectation of God's forgiveness and favor — every time the alarm awakens me to a new day!

Maintaining my relationship with Jesus was so uncomplicated that it shocked me. I once believed that religion was like scaffolding inside an oil tanker: complex to set up and deadly if you missed a single strut or pin. But *anyone* can live a life for Jesus — because *he* holds everything together.

Whenever I slip, he is my lifeline!

❧❧❧

Why was I spared?

One evening when I was young, I was traveling at a high rate of speed and felt that death wobble in my motorcycle's front tire — a biker's nightmare. Suddenly I was skidding along the pavement on my side.

It's the cars around a biker that usually disfigure him. Often drivers following behind a fallen rider do the permanent damage.

When my bike finally stopped grinding sparks on the pavement that night, not a single car was in sight on the highway. I stood up, barely able to walk a straight line after partying all night, and I checked my minor road rash.

My not-so-good friend, the classmate I tossed through the principal's window, didn't fare so well. He overdosed on his demon drug and died. Another old friend (jacked up on meth) met a semi-truck head-on — and I had many friends like these who shared hard living with me, like an infected needle.

How feeble were our bonds, compared to the kinship I have with true brothers and sisters in Christ today!

I've been meth-free for more than a decade now and drug-free for more than eight years. I'm a happily married family man, who builds foundations and walls as a journeyman bricklayer — serving Jesus 24 hours a day.

My mentors and friends at Anthem know where I've been, and many of us share the knowledge of what it means to be lost. God protected us until the moment we were *found.*

On each of our souls Jesus has stamped an indelible imprint of mercy — the very handprint of God.

LIGHT MY WAY HOME
The Story of Angie
Written by Karen Koczwara

Tell me this is all a bad dream.

I slid out of the bed and pulled on my clothes, a fresh wave of humiliation washing over me as I glanced at the stranger beneath the covers. I didn't even know his last name.

I fingered the wad of cash in my pocket, reminding myself that I now had enough to pay three weeks' rent. *Survival, Angie. You did it to survive.*

As I made the trek back home, my feet dragged beneath me, and I felt like someone had just dumped a load of bricks on my shoulders. I glanced up at the Vegas skyline, taking in the fancy casinos that beckoned with their glamour and glitz.

Movie stars played here, yet just a few streets away, there lay another world, the one in which I lived. A world filled with broken dreams, roach-infested dumps, dead-end jobs and cheap booze.

I didn't need to make it into their world; I just didn't want to die a slow death in mine.

And if things didn't start looking up, I wasn't sure I'd have the will to keep on living …

ৡৡৡ

They say home is where the heart is, and for most people, it is true. Home is the place where old memories are reminisced about and new ones are made, where pictures on the wall tell stories of those who've lived inside, where grandchildren find their way to the tattered rope swing that still hangs in the backyard tree. Home is where laughter bursts from the dinner table, where old and young alike gather to recount life's storms and joys, where the wayward child can make his way back after he's wandered off the path and still find a pot of hot soup waiting when he arrives. For most people, finding their way home is the easy part. But for me, the journey back home was long.

I was born in 1963 in Portland, Oregon. My father was in the military, and shortly after my birth, we moved to Michigan. When I turned 2, my mother left my father without his knowledge. When he came home, he found us gone. My mother took me and moved to California, where she knew a few folks. When our destitute conditions did not improve after a couple years, she made the difficult decision to place me in a home with strangers. The couple had three children of their own, and on the weekends, my mother came to visit and gave me special treats.

"Look what I've brought you today, Angie," she announced one Saturday morning when she arrived. She produced a small toy iron from a bag and handed it to me.

I accepted the toy with a shy smile. "Thank you," I whispered. "When are you going to come get me from here, Mommy?"

"Oh, don't you worry. Things won't be like this forever, I promise," she said, patting my head. "We'll get ourselves a nice little place one day soon and be together, okay?"

But as the weeks and months passed, the arrangement did not change. I felt like an outsider as I watched the family interact together, and I longed to have a family and a home of my own. My resentment grew when the other children took my precious belongings and ran away with them. Didn't they know those toys were all I had on this earth to call my own?

One weekend, my mother brought me two little turtles. "I bought them at the pet store," she said excitedly. "Just make sure you feed them and give them water every day."

I held the turtles in my palm and watched them stretch their scrawny legs out of their shells. "I'll take good care of them," I promised.

That night, I made sure to give them plenty of water, just as my mother had instructed. But when I awoke, I discovered to my horror that the turtles were dead! Tears sprang to my eyes as I scooped them up with pity. I was sure one of those bratty kids had done something to my precious pets. Why couldn't they just leave me alone?

I grew more and more quiet and kept to myself. One night, the mother scooped a heaping pile of sauerkraut on my dinner plate and instructed me I could not get up from the table until it was gone. I leaned forward to inspect it, and the pungent smell made my nostril hairs tingle. I yearned for the day my mother could come get me for good and we could enjoy my favorite meals together. She would not make me eat sauerkraut.

I sat there at that table for a long time, staring at my plate until the sun sank into the horizon and the dining room went dark. At last, I stood up, secretly dumped it into the garbage and went off to my room with a rumbling stomach.

It felt like an eternity, but my mother finally came to get me, and we moved into an apartment in Los Angeles, where we lived during my first and second grade years. After a big earthquake, we returned to Oregon, where we stayed with my grandparents for a few months. We then moved to another apartment of our own, where I attended the same school for three consecutive years, from age 9 to 11.

During this time, I attended a program called Missionettes at a local church. Much like Girl Scouts, the program included special activities just for girls. I loved caroling at Christmastime and passing out homemade gifts to elderly residents at retirement homes. But best of all, I loved hearing Bible stories and learning about a God who loved me.

My mother got a decent job, and we moved to a nicer apartment complex, but our situation didn't last long. After the sixth grade, we returned to California and moved in with my aunt for a few months, then with my older cousin. I quickly realized I did not fit in at my new school, and on more than one occasion, my classmates beat me up. I was sick of being the new kid everywhere I went; why couldn't we just settle down?

Just after my 13th birthday, my mother announced we were moving again — this time to Las Vegas. "There are plenty of jobs there, I hear," she said excitedly. "Things will start looking up."

After moving so many times, I had given up on forming deep friendships or connecting with my peers. But Vegas, with its glitzy casinos and clanging slot machines, seemed to offer everyone else a shot at the good life — perhaps all our dreams would come true there as well.

School was just beginning when we arrived, but I didn't bother to enroll myself. Why try to befriend kids I'd probably never see again after a year? We moved in with my mother's friend, but I eventually got caught for truancy and had to enroll in school. It was my second time going through the seventh grade. My mother found a job, and we moved into a nice duplex. I finally felt life was stabilizing.

I went back to Oregon for a couple months to stay with my grandmother and became a live-in babysitter. I enjoyed my new responsibilities and couldn't wait to come home and show my mother how much I'd grown up. I hoped she would see I truly wanted to stay in school, keep my room tidy and help with the household chores.

But when I returned, things weren't as I hoped. On Christmas Day, my mother pulled me into her room and sat me down. Her eyes held the same heavy, defeated look

I'd seen before, and I knew before she even spoke that she had bad news.

"Do you think you might be able to go stay with that lady you lived with in Oregon again?" she asked slowly.

"Why, Mom?" I demanded.

She sighed. "Well, the thing is, Angie, I'm barely making enough to take care of myself. I just can't afford to take care of you, too. I found a studio apartment nearby, but they won't allow anyone under the age of 18 to live there."

I took a deep breath. I was 14 years old. Most girls my age were discussing boys and makeup and the latest school dance, but I was forced to grow up and find myself a place to live. "I'll see what I can do," I stammered.

I called my friend in Oregon, but she was unable to take me in. Desperate, I moved in with a friend. But after a short time, her mother lamented that she could not afford to feed me, and I was forced to move again. This time, a family with seven children took me in. I quickly felt a sense of belonging in their family and became close to the sisters. But it was there that my innocence was stolen when I was molested several times. Life was beginning to feel like one big unfair game.

I was still living with that family when my mother contacted me and told me she was returning to Oregon. "Come with me, Angie," she pleaded. "Vegas isn't all it's cracked up to be. Let's go back home."

Where is home, anyway? I thought to myself sadly. "No, thanks," I told her. "I'm going to stay here."

I have a family now, I told myself. *I have a place to belong.*

I stayed with the family for another year and a half, but my surroundings grew more chaotic. At last, I couldn't take the drinking and the abuse anymore. I left and moved in with my friend again. When we could no longer stay at her place, we moved in with another friend, but that arrangement didn't last long, either.

I moved again into a home with two middle-aged women and offered to clean in exchange for a bed. Within no time, I realized I hadn't improved my situation at all. Drugs and men flowed freely in and out of the doors, and though I tried my best to stay out of it, I soon found myself sucked into the mess. More than once, I awoke to a strange man in my bed who took advantage of me. I cringed as he touched me in places I knew were wrong and wished for the umpteenth time that someone would come and rescue me from this dark little world.

To ease the pain inside, I self-medicated with drugs and found that the temporary high helped me forget all of life's woes. However, things grew darker at the house where I lived, and one day, after being accused of stealing drugs, I'd finally had enough. I called my mother and asked if her offer to move was still open.

"Of course!" she cried.

I returned to Oregon and moved in with my mother, who now worked as a waitress in a lounge next door to her apartment. I was miserable for the first few weeks. I asked my mother to buy me a six-pack of beer and chips and then attempted to drown my miseries on the back patio at night.

"What am I here for, anyway?!" I cried out to the black sky above. "What am I supposed to do with my life?!" But my desperate cries were met with silence, and I polished off the six-pack and bag of chips and continued to cry.

After two months, I got in contact with an old friend and decided to start living again. I obtained a work permit and got a full-time job. One weekend, I attended a concert with my friend and her boyfriend, and they introduced me to his brother. Though we didn't hit it off right away, we soon began dating on and off for the next few months. He couldn't hold down a job, but I invited him to move in with me and my mother, anyhow. It wasn't long before I discovered that living together wasn't working out, and I told him to leave. He did, and I continued working full time and considered attending college. But my plans quickly changed a few months later when I discovered I was pregnant.

The news excited me, and I hoped my boyfriend would be thrilled, too. I didn't consider what it might entail to provide for a child; I just believed that somehow we would be fine. I had been babysitting since I was in grade school and loved being around children. But having one of my own at the age of 17 was a different story. Still, I was determined to keep the baby and do things right. My boyfriend and I would get married and have a family, and perhaps, after years of living on the go, I could finally make a stable life for myself.

After I broke the news to my boyfriend, we moved in with his mother and then went to live with his brother. Finally, we got an apartment of our own. I was excited about starting our life together, but my boyfriend often disappeared for days at a time. I soon learned he was doing drugs and having affairs with other women. Despite his hurtful behavior, I remained determined to make things work.

One day, I learned my father had written me a letter. I had not heard a word from him since my mother left him 18 years earlier. I read the letter, then picked up the phone to call him.

"It's Angie," I said slowly when my father answered.

Our conversation was awkward at first, but we continued to correspond, writing letters back and forth twice a month. It was nice getting to know him. I learned that I had a half sister and brother from his second marriage. I even asked him to give me away at my wedding.

In July 1981, I gave birth to a beautiful little girl, Sarah. She was perfect in every way, and I relished every moment with her, but my bliss was short-lived. My boyfriend's drug habit worsened, and he grew abusive, had multiple affairs and refused to find work.

"This can't go on," I insisted one night after coming home from a long day's work. "You've gotta find a job and shape up."

"You stop telling me what the h*** to do around here, okay?" My boyfriend lunged at me and shoved me against the wall, his eyes dark and fiery as they bore into mine. "I'm sick of your nagging all the time, you stupid b****!"

"I'm sorry, I'm sorry," I whimpered as his hands flew across my face. The impact stung, but I tried to keep from crying. We had a child together and were supposed to get married. I couldn't let him see my fear.

The next morning, my eyes were completely purple. I splashed cold water on my face in the bathroom and stared back at the tired, beat-up girl in the mirror. I'd had enough of his abusive, cheating ways. Unless I wanted to create a life of instability for my daughter like the one I'd grown up in, I needed to put an end to things for good.

"I can't marry you," I told my boyfriend. "You have an addictive personality, and you're ruining both of our lives. The wedding's off."

"What the h*** are you talking about?" he demanded. "Are you crazy?"

No, but you are, I thought to myself, my stomach turning as I walked away.

We called off the wedding, but a few months later, to my surprise, my father showed up at my door. I had forgotten I'd written him, asking him to give me away on my big day. I didn't have the heart to tell him I'd called the wedding off, so I quickly threw together a wedding in two days. Our next-door neighbor, a pastor, married us in the courtyard of our apartments.

It was nice to finally meet my father in person, and to my surprise, we enjoyed each other's company. He had the same sarcastic humor as me and used the same animated hand motions when he spoke. It was hard to believe nearly two decades had passed since we'd seen each other.

"It's great to see you again, Angie," my father said tenderly when we'd cleaned our plates. "It seems like you've made a good life for yourself. And you've made me a grandfather, too!"

I wasn't sure about all that. I didn't have the heart to tell him all my sad stories, how I'd spent my childhood moving from home to home, a stranger amidst other people's families, all because my mother had left him when I was 2. "I'm doing pretty well," I said at last, mustering a smile.

My husband and I moved to a nearby town, and he got a job and decided to quit using drugs. For a little while, life resumed a normal pace.

"I want another baby," my husband told me. "Are you ready?"

I could see that he was trying to make a better life for our family, so I agreed. Soon, I became pregnant, and my husband slipped back into his old behavior, doing drugs and cheating on me. In 1985, I gave birth to a son, Christopher. I began working three jobs, including my husband's, as he often failed to show up for work. Exhaustion overwhelmed me as I worked seven days a week while caring for our young children.

As Thanksgiving neared, I grew especially sick and went to the doctor.

"You have double pneumonia," he informed me

grimly. "If this medication doesn't work, you could die."

The shocking diagnosis was a wake-up call. I finally took a break from work to rest, and after I got better, I quit two of the jobs. But the insanity in our house remained as my husband continued to abuse drugs. Instead of leaving him, however, I decided we simply needed a change of scenery.

"We need to go where the jobs are, and the jobs are in Vegas," I told him. "I'm going, and if you want to come, you can."

In January 1986, we moved our family to Las Vegas, hoping that the desert air might offer some hope. I got a job as a cook at a bar, and though my husband got a job there as well, he often skipped out on his shifts, leaving me to cover for him to save face. He continued abusing drugs, smoking crack at all hours of the day instead of working to pay the bills. At night, when I fell into bed, exhausted from my head to my toes, he forced himself on me.

"Not tonight," I begged. "I'm so tired! Besides, I need to get the pill first. I don't want to get pregnant."

But he pulled me toward him, anyway. I didn't have the physical strength to fight him off, so I reluctantly submitted.

My heart sank as I realized that it did not matter where we lived. My husband was not going to change his ways. I continued to give in to his physical demands, and within weeks, I learned I was pregnant again. Terrified to bring another child into our chaotic life, I opted to have an abortion. It seemed like the only logical choice.

Not long after, my husband broke our truck. Due to lack of transportation, we both lost our jobs. He sold the truck and decided to take that money, pack up and move back to Oregon, leaving me behind with no car and no means to support myself. *Good riddance,* I thought as I watched him go.

I had a friend watch the children while I walked for miles to obtain emergency government assistance. I was so happy to receive $150. I found a run-down duplex to rent for $75 per week and used every penny I had gotten to pay for two weeks' rent.

Every day, I walked the streets of Vegas in search of work. As my worn shoes pounded the pavement, I fought back tears. I had never had a problem finding a job before. As a last resort, I found a job at a wine club, where I was forced to slip into lingerie and sip non-alcoholic wine with the patrons. My friend watched my children while I worked the 10 p.m. to 6 a.m. shift. The work was demeaning, and I hated every minute of it, but it was better than nothing, I reasoned. I made enough to pay rent the first couple of weeks and continued to look for better work during the day. But once again, the money soon ran dry, and I scrambled to come up with the following week's rent. The owner of the wine club approached me with a proposal.

"How much do you want?" he asked.

I gulped. "Seventy-five dollars." I was desperate. If I didn't do this, my children and I would literally end up on the streets.

"Why so much?" he pressed.

But I didn't respond. He agreed to the amount, and I reluctantly went to bed with him. Tears pricked my eyes, and I hated every second of the encounter. *I've reached a new low,* I thought grimly to myself when it was over. *What am I going to do?* I was able to pay the next week's rent, but I'd have to fork over another $75 the following week. I was making next to nothing at the wine club, and I despised working there. One evening, a man came in and approached me seductively. "I'm staying at a hotel just down the street," he whispered in my ear. "I'll give you $300 if you come back with me."

My chest tightened at his words. I needed the money badly, and $300 would cover three weeks' rent and plenty of food for the children. I accepted his offer and followed him back to his hotel that night, where I gave myself to another man I would never see again. I felt sick as I made my way home when the sun came up. *What have I become?* I thought with disdain. I'd heard about the prostitutes who walked the streets of Vegas, offering up a good time. I just never thought I would be one of them.

My husband called one day to offer me money. "I know you need my help," he said.

"Then wire me the money," I said firmly. I didn't want him back, but I was down to my last few dollars, and I did need his help.

To my surprise, he did as I asked. I was excited, for the

LIGHT MY WAY HOME

funds allowed me to not have to work at the wine club. I was even more surprised when he wired money a second time.

"What's your address?" he asked finally.

I hesitated, not wanting him to show up at my door.

"I'm not gonna come there," he added, sensing my apprehension.

I believed him and recited my address. He showed up in Vegas a few days later. When he arrived, he begged me to take him back and threatened to take the children if I didn't oblige. I tried to please him for two days, but at last I couldn't stand it any longer.

"Forget it! I can't take you back!" I cried.

He freaked out momentarily and then calmed down. "Fine. I'm leaving. Don't worry, I'm not gonna take the kids." And he walked out the door.

When I arrived home early one morning after work a couple days later, I found the apartment completely ransacked. Dresser drawers had been yanked out and tossed onto the ground, and clothes were strewn about. "Oh, God!" I screamed.

"I tried to stop him," cried my friend, who'd been babysitting. "But he just stormed in and went nuts! He took the kids a few hours ago."

He really meant it. He took the kids back to Oregon. Terror gripped me as I pictured my kids being whisked away in the middle of the night. I called the police, but after I explained that we were still married, they informed me that he hadn't technically kidnapped them, and there wasn't much they could do. I tried over and over to reach my husband, but he suddenly went missing. I contacted everyone I knew, but no one had any information. I finally learned that he was hiding in the woods. Oregon is covered with woods, and my heart sank as I worried that I might never see my children again. Worse yet, I didn't even have enough money to get to Oregon, even if I wanted to. My life was spiraling out of control, and I didn't have a clue how to fix it.

The children had been my only reason to live. With them gone, I began to question my existence. What did it matter if I worked anymore? Maybe I should just curl up and shut the world out.

I began hanging out with an old friend from my teens. He presented me with mainlining drugs. I'd never touched serious drugs before, but I figured I didn't have much to live for anymore. As he slipped the needle into my vein, I hoped it would quickly numb my pain so I would not have to think about what a mess I'd made of my life. I stared up at the dingy ceiling as the darkness enclosed me and wondered if there could be any more to this miserable existence. Was I really meant to spend the rest of my days in a state of desperate loneliness?

I lived next door to the drug cook and began selling drugs myself. One day, I woke up feeling especially lousy. After taking a test, I discovered to my horror that I was pregnant. My stomach churned as I glanced around the empty apartment we would soon be evicted from. How could I possibly bring another child into the world in these conditions? After securing some money, I made an appointment at an abortion clinic and decided I had no choice but to terminate the pregnancy.

"I'm not sure if you're aware, but you're already 15 weeks along," the technician at the clinic informed me as I sat across from him.

"Fifteen weeks?" I sputtered. "But that's impossible …" I thought about the ultrasounds I'd had during my first two pregnancies. I'd reasoned away my first abortion by saying it was just a tiny pollywog, not a real formed human being, but a 15-week-old baby … well, that was a different story. I took a deep breath and clenched my fists, reeling at the news.

"So, basically, you're too far along to have an abortion," the technician continued.

"Too far along," I repeated numbly. I stared down at my belly, already slightly bulging under my shirt. I should have known weeks ago. What was I going to do now?!

I walked home that night and glanced up at the starry sky beneath the bright Vegas lights. "Oh, God, oh, God, oh, God!" I cried out into the air. "Please don't let this baby be addicted! Please let this baby be all right! I promise I will stop doing everything and take care of myself." I didn't know much about God, but I believed he existed, and I needed his help more than ever right now. I was about to embark on the scariest ride of my life.

I immediately quit using drugs and tried to take care of myself. As my belly expanded, I wondered how I'd be able to provide for this child when it arrived. I sometimes scarcely had enough food to eat. However, I believed this baby was meant to be, and for the first time in a while, I had a reason to live again. I desperately missed my other two children and dreamed about them nearly every night. My current living conditions were less than ideal, but I hoped one day soon I could be reunited with my children and work everything out.

One chilly February afternoon, I waddled the seven blocks to the doctor's office for my second visit. I hadn't been going to see the doctor on a regular basis, but my due date was just around the corner. I was thrilled when the doctors agreed I could have a natural birth after the C-section I had with my son. As I got off the table to go home, I felt a huge gush. When I looked down, I saw fluid dripping beneath my legs. My water had just broken! I cleaned it up and tried to walk back home, but I only made it a block before calling for a ride. I was starving and wanted to enjoy one last meal at home before having the baby.

When I got home, I ate a chef's salad and took a short nap. When I awoke, my contractions were stronger. It was officially time to have the baby! I called for a ride again and made it to the hospital in time.

At 1 a.m., my daughter entered the world. As the doctors placed her tiny pink body on my chest, I marveled at her perfect little features, unable to believe I'd almost made the decision to end her life before it even started. I knew she was a gift from God, though I hadn't a clue what I'd done to deserve something so beautiful and good.

"I shall call you Leah," I told my newborn daughter as I gazed into her face. I glanced around at my empty hospital room. There were no balloons, no flowers, no welcoming party of eager grandparents just waiting to take a peek at the new child. With my mother in Oregon, my husband still in hiding and still no real friends in my new town, it should have been one of the loneliest days of my life. Yet I had a wonderful little being in my arms, and somehow just looking at her convinced me that everything was going to be all right. It was not until I fell asleep that morning that I realized the date: February 14. Valentine's Day.

I moved into a low-cost apartment with Leah's father, whom I continued to date, and got a job as a cook at a bar. When Leah was 6 months old, my estranged husband called one day out of the blue. "I'll give you back Sarah," he offered.

Relief washed over me at his words. "Don't split them up. I want both the kids back," I insisted. He hung up before I could say anything else. I was devastated, as I still had no idea where he was. A couple months later, he called again and offered to give Sarah back. I was used to his games and manipulation, but I was also confident it was only a matter of time before he relented and gave both children back.

I agreed to his terms and welcomed my daughter back with open arms. Beyond grateful to have her in my arms again, I carried her all the way through the airport to the baggage claim. At nearly 6 years old, she was far too young to understand the painful circumstances surrounding our situation. Someday, I would tell her.

In 1989, my estranged husband called again and agreed to give my 4-year-old son back to me. I was elated to be reunited with all my children at last.

"We will have to get a divorce and put the children in my custody if you want to see them again," I told him. The arrangement was the only way I could trust him to visit them. I was tired of his lies and his manipulation, but I didn't want to keep the children from their father. Vegas may not exactly have been the fresh start I was looking for, but it was certainly a relief to be away from his abusiveness.

I got a new job at another restaurant run by a nice Jewish man. He owned a few lounges around the city and appeared very successful and confident. Whenever I spoke with him, I went tongue-tied, as he intimidated me. I was grateful for the work, though, and determined that I would do my best to provide for my family. With three kids crammed into one tiny room, I needed to find a way to better our situation.

One day, my boss shared something with me. "You want to know why I am so happy and successful, Angie?" he said. "It is because I have been reading a new, very motivating book. In a nutshell, I am learning that our mind is a very powerful tool, and we can control our own destiny through effective use of our mind rather than letting others control us. Studying these concepts is changing my life!"

I raised an eyebrow. "Really? I've never heard of it." I thought of my estranged husband, who had manipulated me for so many years. I then thought of my current lifestyle, hardly the picture of success. Was my boss onto something? Was it possible I could control my own destiny? "I'd like to know more," I agreed. "Where can I find the book?"

"I'll give you a copy," he replied. "I think you're going to find that it's really going to change your life. You're a smart girl, Angie, I can tell. You just need the tools to move forward."

The next day, I hopped on my 10-speed bike and rode off to work, popping in the 7-Eleven for an herbal energy drink to get me through my shift. On the way into the restaurant, I stopped at the bar for a shot of tequila to top things off. As I rushed through my duties, I thought about my boss' words. What did I have to lose by reading the book?

I picked up the book my boss had given me and began thumbing through it. "You are not a victim," the book emphasized over and over. "You control your destiny. It is the choices you make that affect your future." For the first time in a long while, things made sense. Though I had always been a self-starter, a go-getter and a hard worker, I had allowed myself to be controlled by abusive men and blamed others for the way my life had turned out. Was it possible I was the one responsible for where I was?

One day during my shift, I popped into the walk-in fridge to make a plate of nachos. I squirted the sour cream on the chips and then grabbed the bottle of salsa as usual. But as I began to shake the bottle, the lid flew off, and salsa spewed everywhere.

"Who did this?!" I screamed, furious that someone had left the lid unscrewed and created such a mess.

My boss, who was stocking the shelves next to me, looked up and smirked. "That was your fault, Angie," he said, shaking his head. "You should have checked the lid."

"What are you talking about? No, whoever didn't put the lid back on, it's his fault. I always put the lid back on!" I retorted. I began to grumble as I mopped up the mess and put the order of nachos out. The rest of the night, I replayed the scenario in my head, arguing to myself that the mess was not my fault. But the next time I stepped back into the walk-in to make another plate of nachos, I suddenly realized that my boss was right. The mess was all my fault.

I went home that night and thought more about the incident as I read the book. *My mother rejected me. My father rejected me. Life has been unfair.* This was the broken record that had replayed in my mind for years. I was a victim ... wasn't I? There was just nothing I could do about my life or my future ... or was there?

From that moment on, I always checked the lid on the salsa.

≈≈≈

My husband officially divorced me in 1990, and I was granted full custody of both our children. I was relieved to have him out of my life and glad he would only see the kids for visitation once a year.

A pastor from a church down the road showed up on my doorstep one day. He invited us to church, but I politely declined. "No, thanks. I learned all that Bible stuff when I was a kid," I replied. "Thanks, anyway."

My kids hovered behind me, their eyes wide and eager. The pastor smiled at them and then nodded at me. "Well, we have a van that transports kids to church every Sunday if your children ever want to go," he said. "We'd be more than happy to pick them up."

I reluctantly agreed to let my children go to church in the van. For the next few months, I waved goodbye to them as the vehicle pulled up at our little four-plex and drove off. I remembered being picked up in a van and going to church when I was a kid. The children came home eager to share the Bible stories and songs they'd learned in church.

"Please come with us, Mom," they begged.

"Not this weekend. Mommy's too tired," I told them.

My relationship with my boyfriend grew more tumultuous. His drinking was out of control, and mine wasn't far behind. I plodded through my days, often hung over, downing my energy drinks and working long hours, only to get up and do it all over again.

One morning, I woke up and thought to myself, *I wonder what it's like to go to church as an adult?* The thought surprised me, as I hadn't given church much thought until then.

I bounded out of bed, got dressed and decided to go to church. My boyfriend agreed to go with me. When we arrived at a small older office building, I wondered if we had the wrong address. But the minute I stepped inside, I realized I was in the right place. I took a seat in the back, suddenly self-conscious of my bad teeth and straggly hair. Wasn't church for folks who had it all together, not messed-up girls like me?

Just as I began to shift in my seat and wonder if I'd made a mistake in coming, the pastor's wife took a seat at the piano and began playing a beautiful hymn, "The Old Rugged Cross." As she ran her fingers over the keys and the voices filled up that little room, tears began to stream down my cheeks out of nowhere as I read the words from the hymn book.

"On a hill far away, stood an old rugged cross, the emblem of suffering and shame. And I love that old cross, where the dearest and best, for a world of lost sinners was slain ..."

My tears turned to heavy sobs as the hymn continued. *A world of lost sinners.* That was me! *I know why my life sucks,* I realized. *I'm living a life of sin!*

According to the Bible, sin was the wrong things we all did in our life. No one was exempt from messing up. I had learned about sin when I attended Missionettes and heard the Bible stories as a young girl. Suddenly, it was all so very clear. I had heard the stories about Jesus as a child, I had cried out to God many times as an adult and I had certainly always believed he existed. But I had never made a choice to invite him into my life.

He had been like a long-lost acquaintance I called on every once in a while when things got really bad, but I'd never truly made him my best friend. I'd sought out answers in books, but that hadn't been the answer, either. Booze, drugs and men had only drained my soul, not filled it. There was only one thing I needed in my life right now, I realized, and that was Jesus!

As the pastor's message came to an end, he asked if anyone in the room would like to invite Jesus into his or her heart. "It does not matter what you have done or where you have come from," he added, as though speaking right to me. "God loved each of us so much that he sent his son, Jesus, to earth to pay the price for the wrong things we've done on that old rugged cross we sang about this morning. If you would like a fresh start with him, he is ready and waiting with open arms to give you that peace you've been searching your whole life for. By inviting him into your life and confessing your sins, you can experience a lasting relationship with him and spend eternity in heaven. Please come forward if you'd like to pray and ask Jesus to change your life."

I sat glued to my seat, my cheeks stained with tears. I glanced over at my boyfriend, who was blocking my path to the aisle. I did not go up to the altar that morning, but I knew there was something different in me at that moment. There was light inside of me where darkness had once been, a newfound hope where there had been despair. I was suddenly alive!

I practically floated out to the parking lot afterward. From the outside, that little church was just an ordinary building, but something extraordinary had just happened for me inside. As I walked home, I glanced up at the sky, and somehow it seemed brighter, too. I had just found Jesus, and I knew my life would never be the same again.

The next morning, as I washed my face, I glanced up in the mirror. My teeth were still troublesome, and my hair was still in disarray. But despite my disheveled look, I felt beautiful from the inside out. When I got to work, I dropped something on the ground, but instead of curse words flying out of my mouth, I muttered, "Darn."

"What did you say?" my co-worker asked, surprised.

"I said darn," I replied, laughing.

I didn't drink the whole week, but by the weekend, I reasoned that I had been good and could have just one drink. But as the alcohol went down, it didn't taste so good anymore. *I don't want this life anymore,* I told myself that Saturday morning when I woke up hung over. *I am going to church on Sunday, and nothing is going to stop me!*

I showed up at the little church again the next morning and sat in the same place. When the pastor asked if anyone would like to come forward to invite Jesus into his or her heart, I practically leapt out of my seat and headed down the aisle. This time, as I talked to God, it was more than just a desperate shout out into the sky. I poured out my heart to him, asking him to forgive me for the lifestyle I'd been living and thanking him for loving me just as I was. *Help me, God, to live the way you want me to from now on,* I prayed. *I know it won't always be easy, but I now know that you are the only answer. For me, there's no turning back.*

I gave up booze, smoking and cursing for good. I began reading my Bible, and the stories came alive as I flipped through the pages. Some people believe the Bible is nothing but a rule book, but I came to see it as much more than that — as God's love story to us. And by reading it and praying, I could grow closer to him and understand how he wanted me to live. The book I'd read said I could control my own destiny, but I knew even the best laid plans could fall flat. The God of the Bible was the only one truly in control, and if I followed him, I could find true peace even in the midst of hardship.

As I continued to pore over my Bible, I read about a man named Saul who had once hated anyone who loved God. But God had radically changed his heart, and he had changed his name to Paul and spent the rest of his life sharing God's love with others. "I want to be like Paul, God," I prayed. "You did something radical inside of me and turned the darkness in my heart to light. I want everyone to know I am changed."

To show everyone I was a new person, I decided to get baptized the day after my birthday. I participated in a special ceremony in which the pastor dunked me in water to represent Jesus giving me a new life. Friends from my new church cheered and hugged me as I rose from the water. The Bible said I was a new creation in Christ, and I truly felt that way that day.

"I want to get married," I told my boyfriend after the holidays. I had been praying and knew God did not want me living with someone I was not married to. My boyfriend was still an alcoholic, but I hoped he, too, would change his ways and find hope in God.

My boyfriend agreed to marry me, and we said I do in March 1993. We found a beautiful four-bedroom two-story house in an expensive neighborhood, and we were able to rent it for only $700 per month. After years of living in slum-like conditions, I nearly had to pinch myself as we moved our things in. I thanked God for his kindness and his provision.

But not long after we settled into our new place, my world began to unravel again. My husband left me, and my oldest daughter ran away from home. I had been working four 10-hour shifts at the restaurant, but with no one to care for my younger kids, I was forced to quit my job. The car I'd worked so hard to purchase was repossessed, and the money began to run out. I knew being a Christian did not mean I was promised a perfect life, but I had not been prepared for such hardship all at once.

"God, what am I going to do now?" I cried out. While panic would have once overwhelmed me, I now rested in his peace, knowing that even though this felt like rock bottom, I was not alone. God was on my side, and he would get me through this.

In-home daycare, I felt God prompt me.

I looked into business licensing and decided to take the leap and open an in-home daycare. My first clients were struggling single mothers who could only afford to pay a few dollars per week. But I wanted to be a blessing to them, so I took in their children and trusted that God would provide the rest. Each month was terribly tight. We lived off of cucumber sandwiches, literally relying on God for our daily bread. At night, I knelt down and cried out to God, asking him to provide all of our needs. And as I read my Bible, a verse continued to pop out at me. Luke 12:31 read, "But seek his kingdom, and these things will be given to you as well." *Okay, God,* I prayed. *I'm going to keep putting you first.*

The following year, my husband asked if I'd take him back, and I agreed. He still drank heavily, but I wanted to be obedient to God and chose to forgive him. When he returned, however, the State forced me to re-do my daycare paperwork, and I encountered more bad news.

"I'm afraid he's got a bad criminal record," the detective handling our case informed me. "If you take him back in, you'll be forced to shut down your daycare."

God, is this just another test? I prayed, desperate for answers. *Should I choose my husband over my business and risk everything I'd worked so hard for these past two years?* After praying, I decided to close down the daycare. But not long after I did, my husband and I separated again, and I was left all alone with hardly a penny to my name.

The next year was one of the most difficult of my life. I moved several times, from one roach-infested house to another, and took odd jobs cleaning, painting and working in retail. But each month, things only got worse. I began to think about Oregon and wondered if I should go back. I often told people, "You can't pay me to go back to Oregon." I'd never planned on returning, but maybe God was trying to move me on. How would I know for sure?

One Saturday night, I poured my heart out to God, asking him to clearly show me if going back to Oregon was the right decision.

The next morning, I showed up at church. I'd left the little church to attend a bigger church down the road, and so far, I had enjoyed the new friends I'd met there. I'd even had the opportunity to teach children's Sunday school classes and go on mission trips to Mexico, a new and fun experience for me. Now, as I sat in my seat, a couple in the front stood up and walked straight toward me.

"I see a light in you, and you are surrounded by trees," the woman told me boldly. "You are not supposed to be here!"

I stared at her, taken aback by her words. Just recently, my best friend had said to me, "I just don't see you here in Vegas, Angie. You don't fit in!" I thought of the dusty desert landscape in Vegas. *I was surrounded by trees?* Suddenly, I knew without a doubt what I needed to do. It was time to head back to Oregon, where I'd first come from.

Two weeks later, I packed what few belongings we owned into a little U-Haul to tow behind my car. We set off on the long drive, but after arriving in Tonopah, the car died. I rented a 14-foot truck and transferred our belongings into it. My young daughter carefully carried her fishbowl as we drove away. I had $200 to get me all the way to Oregon, and I knew most of that would be eaten up by gas. As usual, I prayed, asking God to get us there by some miracle.

We made it from Tonopah to Reno, when it began snowing so hard that we had to use some of our precious funds for a cheap hotel. The following day, we headed over the treacherous summit, and more snow began to fall. I noticed semi-trucks lined up alongside the road, and my heart sank. *God, just please get us to a hotel for the night,* I prayed.

"The summits are all closed from California to Oregon," the hotel clerk informed me.

My heart sank again. But the next morning, the sun shone brightly when I awoke, and we hopped back in the truck and made the rest of the trip. As the thick green Northwest trees came into view, I prayed once again, "God, if this is your will for me to be here, that's all I care about." At that very moment, a dove flew right in front of my window. I remembered the story of Noah's Ark in the Bible, how God had sent a dove to represent his promises. A huge smile crept to my face, as I realized that no matter how uncertain my future might be, God had a plan for me here.

After a long, precarious four-day trip, we finally arrived in Portland. God was faithful to provide all our needs. I temporarily moved in with my mother, and during my stay, I began to share Jesus with her.

"I just want you to know that I've forgiven you for everything in our past," I told her sincerely.

After a few months, I secured a place to live and had found sales work shortly after I arrived. I trusted God to provide, and I was able to enroll my kids in a private school. A scholarship helped to pay a portion of their way. Things were beginning to fall into place, and as the weeks passed, I remained confident that I'd made the right decision by leaving Vegas behind.

I found a church similar to the one I'd attended in Vegas and began taking the kids. I was a completely different woman than the girl who had moved away from Oregon years ago, yet God was still working on me inside. One day, during my prayer time, God gave me a picture in my mind of a little Pilgrim slave girl ironing clothes. In the background behind her, I saw a beautiful girl. Slowly, the Pilgrim girl faded away, and the beautiful girl came into focus.

You are no longer a slave, I felt God say to me. *You are a daughter of the King.*

Tears spilled down my cheeks at this beautiful picture God had shown me. I'd spent my whole life feeling inadequate, despite all my hard work and motivated attitude. Whenever I spoke to anyone of any stature or education, I fumbled my words and felt my cheeks flush. I had even succumbed to the manipulation of unstable men because I felt I did not deserve anyone better. But I now saw myself as God saw me — his beautiful daughter, a prized piece of art. I had worth because I belonged to the Master who created me, and I was valuable to him. Best of all, he loved me just as I was.

తతత

The woman on the corner could have been me. She glanced up with weary eyes — her leathery skin told a story of a life filled with hardship and pain. I knelt beside her and handed her a kit filled with personal items I hoped she could use. The woman, like many others here on the streets of downtown Portland, was trying to start a new life after being released from prison. But it would not be easy.

"God loves you, and though you may not feel like it sometimes, he does have a good plan for your life," I shared with the woman before I left. "May I pray with you?"

She agreed, and I prayed, asking God to bless the woman's life and give her the peace I'd found in him so many years before. My friends at church often said that they felt God's presence when I prayed, and I thanked God for this gift, as I knew it came straight from him. When I stood, I saw a flicker of hope in the woman's eyes and the hint of a smile on her lips.

The past decade had been filled with a mixture of

hardship and blessing. I'd succeeded at my sales job and received recognition and promotions. But my heart broke when my oldest daughter went astray for a time and dabbled with unhealthy things. The Bible verse Jeremiah 31:16 reads, "'Restrain your voice from weeping and your eyes from tears, for your work will be rewarded,' declares the Lord. 'They will return from the land of the enemy.'" Since inviting Jesus into my heart, I had come to believe in the power of prayer, and I had prayed this prayer over and over for my children and believed it. He had answered my prayer and worked a wonderful change in my daughter's heart!

I had found a place to belong at a wonderful church, called Anthem Church, where I'd had the opportunity to teach the children and work with the women's prison ministry for a year. Anthem offered a fresh start for all, no matter where they had come from or what their past entailed. I praised God that he had strengthened my relationship with my mother. She now lives with me and attends church, along with all of my children and my six grandchildren. Best of all, each of them has invited Jesus into their heart.

God restored my relationship with my father, and in 2011, he invited me to Texas to spend a week with him and his sister. I'd also been able to share God's love with my two ex-husbands and pray over them. God had given me the ability to forgive easily, and I'd never harbored any resentment toward the men who had hurt me in my past. This allowed me to live freely, without carrying a heavy burden on my shoulders. It also helped me to see them as God saw them — broken people in need of his love.

At a Christmas service at Anthem, the pastor encouraged us to dedicate an ornament on the tree to the memory of a loved one. I stepped up and wrote "third child," in honor of the child I'd aborted in Las Vegas. Though I knew God had forgiven me for that act, I had never acknowledged the child as a real person until then. Suddenly, I pictured that third child sitting on Jesus' lap in heaven, and I wept tears of sadness and release. God was so good — even in sorrow, he could bring joy.

As I finished ministering to the homeless women and headed back to my car that night, I glanced up at the Portland night sky behind the downtown buildings and thought of Vegas. Years before, I had walked those lonely streets, looking for work, destitute, afraid and hopeless. But I met Jesus there in that city, and he filled me with life again and gave me a new, happy heart. I am grateful for where I am now, but I will never forget where I came from. Without God, I found myself wandering. It took a while for me to learn that if I held onto him, I'd find rest and a place to belong. And I will always remember that long road that led me back home.

THE MYSTERIOUS TREE
The Story of Mike Bates
Written by Marty Minchin

"Whose van is that?" I asked my dad after pulling into my parents' driveway in Minnesota. I'd been living in California for a few months, and they hadn't mentioned buying a new vehicle.

"I borrowed it to haul some stuff," he replied nonchalantly, glancing back at the house. "I have to take it back in the morning. You want to go with me?"

"Sure." I didn't have any other plans for my overnight visit. My new friend Eric and I were on our way to Madison, Wisconsin, where the church I'd recently become wrapped up in, and which my parents regarded as a cult, had assigned us to recruit new members on college campuses.

Eric, Mom, Dad and I loaded into the van the next morning to return it to Bob Jordan, a longtime family friend. Two beefy guys leaning against a telephone pole eyed us as we turned into Bob's driveway.

Before the van had even rolled to a stop, the side doors flew open. The men slid in, sandwiching Eric and me on the bench seat and squashing us between their hefty frames. The doors slammed shut as Dad backed out of the driveway.

"What's going on?" I leaned forward and asked quizzically, but my parents stared straight ahead, and Dad gave the van some gas. "What the heck, Dad!"

Come on, you're not that surprised. Thoughts programmed in my head took over. *We warned you. These are agents out to stop you from completing your mission, and you are chosen by God to do this work. They'll deceive your parents. Don't trust anybody.*

The van squealed out onto the highway, and I could hear some murmuring from the front about Eric. They didn't plan to take him along for this ride.

"Get him out," my dad called back to the two men. We pulled over on the shoulder of the highway, where Eric was to be ejected.

Eric, however, was okay with being kidnapped by my parents and two thugs. He grabbed the back of the seat as my mom, who'd come from the outside, tried to pull him off while one thug worked to unclench Eric from the seat.

"Don't fight," my dad barked back at me after I kicked the back of his seat.

I could barely answer, as my 220-pound seatmate now was lying on top of me. My mom shrieked as the van door slammed on her arm, but she pulled it out and jumped back in the passenger seat.

We left Eric, bewildered, on the side of the road as we sped off toward West Virginia.

❧ ❧ ❧

THE MYSTERIOUS TREE

My parents met at Iowa Wesleyan College in Mount Pleasant, Iowa, in the early 1950s. What made their meeting and marriage so noteworthy was that my mother is white, a mixture of Irish and Welsh, and my dad is African-American, the son of domestic workers. My mom, I imagine, savored a little of the rebellion in this relationship, as a mixed-race couple in the 1950s was not just unusual, but shunned. Interracial marriage was illegal in some states until 1967, when the Supreme Court struck down laws preventing people of different races from marrying.

My parents' union was not without sacrifice. My mom was kicked out of her sorority for dating my dad, and her parents refused to attend the wedding. My dad's folks weren't too happy about the marriage, either. But my parents were determined to be together, and after they married, they moved to the south side of Minneapolis. They soon had two kids — me and my sister, who is two years older than me. I have light brown skin and wavy black hair, and in the Scandinavian communities of Western Minnesota, my sister and I did not fit in.

We settled into a primarily white neighborhood in Minneapolis, where my parents eventually bought a house. They had approached the same real estate agent separately about purchasing the house, and they went with the significantly lower price that my mom was quoted. My parents took teaching jobs at different schools, and my dad, who taught biology and science, was the only African-American teacher at his. Neither the black nor the white communities welcomed our mixed-race family, and my mom recalls one woman at a breakfast for teachers' wives looking at my sister and me and asking, "Now whose little pickaninnies are those?"

Racism ran like an undercurrent in Minnesota, where the jabs and pokes were subtle. No one yelled in our faces or openly insulted us. We just weren't included.

My family spent a lot of time at home during the school year. It wasn't until I was an adult that I realized black people gathered and did things socially, as we had never been included in groups of either race.

In Minnesota, I attended a school across town that dismissed late in the afternoon, and by the time I got home, the neighborhood kids were already inside doing homework.

Summers, however, were a different story. My parents' teaching jobs provided three months of vacation, and by the time June arrived, they were itching to get out of the city. One of my dad's coworkers recommended that we visit Otter Tail Lake in Northern Minnesota, where the high winds regularly crossing the large body of water made it a popular place to sail.

On one of our first visits, my dad tried to chat with a fellow campground visitor, a white guy leaning up against his Volkswagen Microbus. The man's black dog, Sam, which I'm sure was short for Sambo, sat at his feet, and his shotgun leaned against the vehicle.

"I'm interested in getting one of those buses," my dad said, trying a friendly approach. "How do you like it?"

The man tilted his head and looked my dad over. "I like it fine," he drawled. "But I don't care for you very much."

"Oh, great," my dad muttered, and at a loss for what else to say, we walked away. I could tell he was upset as he marched straight to the campground owner's office. The night before, my dad had overheard some conversations among our fellow campers who weren't pleased to be set up next to a mixed-race family, and the Microbus owner had pushed him over the edge.

"We haven't been made to feel very welcome here," my dad explained to the campground owner. "We just want to camp and fish here, like everyone else. Can you move us to a different campsite?"

The owner readily obliged, switching us to a nice open space in the back of the campsite with no one right up around us. But he had another solution that was even better.

"I have some property for sale over here." He pointed across the lake. "Only one other lot has been sold there."

We understood his meaning. If my parents bought the lot, they'd be one of the first property owners in that section of the lake. If potential buyers didn't like the fact that we owned the land, they didn't have to buy there. We were almost guaranteed neighbors who were okay with our family.

My parents soon owned a big piece of property with a nice sandy beach, and they built an A-frame cabin there. It became our summer home, and we had our side of the lake mostly to ourselves because our neighbors only came up on the weekends. Otter Tail Lake summers were peaceful, relaxing — and isolated.

❧ ❧ ❧

"Hey, you guys want to head over to the Hurdy Gurdy for happy hour?"

I often felt alone, and invitations to hang out with friends were rare, so I jumped at the chance to hang out with my college orientation leader at Mankato State College in Minnesota. We headed off to the new saloon in town and settled into its brightly colored seats as music from a live band filled the room.

The drinking age was 18 in the early 1970s, and I relished the chance to loosen up with a few beers and talk with my new friends. Alcohol and pot, I learned, were great equalizers, and by my third year in college, I knew that you never went anywhere without a six-pack of beer and some weed. When a group of people got together and smoked pot, everyone was mellow, and everyone was in love with everybody.

I met Marvin when I was a freshman, and he invited me to a few fraternity parties. Our group was small, maybe 15 or 20 guys, and I enjoyed sitting down and having deep philosophical conversations with them. While college wasn't without its racial moments, where fellow students casually threw out the "N" word or decided they didn't like a band because the musicians were African-American, in the midst of the partying and banter, I formed a few solid friendships. One fraternity brother invited me home with his family over Easter one year. I was even the best man in my roommate's wedding.

My grand plan in life was to teach school for a few years, then return to college for a master's degree and go into counseling. I liked the idea of having summers off, and I had always thought that counselors had the coolest job in the school. With a bachelor's degree in industrial education, I got a job teaching graphic arts at a magnet trade school in Hanska, Minnesota, a rural town with a population of 400.

I found a little house in the newspaper classifieds that looked like an ideal place to live, so I called up the property owner.

"Yeah, sure," he told me, his accent distinctly German. "Come on by."

He said he was at the house, which was only two blocks away. I drove around the corner to meet him.

The front of the house was dominated by a large picture window covered with a reflective film. As I walked up to the door, I realized that I couldn't see in, but anyone inside could see out. I knocked on the door. No answer. I knocked again. Still nothing. I had *just* called the guy at this house. I knew he was inside.

I leaned over to peer in the window and caught my reflection; my Afro and sun-tanned skin stared back at me. There was no question as to why the man wouldn't answer the door.

꙾꙾꙾

I found an apartment over a store 10 miles away on Main Street in Madelia. It only served to intensify my lonely existence, as I had no neighbors or friends to hang out with. I was still loosely dating my college girlfriend, Ellie, but she had moved to Dallas with her sister, and we only saw each other a few times a year and talked on the phone once a week. The people I did meet who were close in age spent their free time drinking and taking downers, which seemed dumb to me. Why would you want to spend your weekend in a near-catatonic state?

When a few girls I knew from college called unexpectedly, I was ecstatic.

"We'll take you out and introduce you to some people!" they trilled. I happily piled into their car, unconcerned about our destination.

We headed out into the country as the sun set, finally arriving at a double-wide trailer in the dark. I wondered what I was getting myself into as we walked up to it.

The door slowly opened, and smoke poured out into the cold night. I peered inside, but it was so thick I couldn't make out what was going on inside. Like a scene from a bad movie, a hand extended out of the smoky haze, two fingers clutching a joint. I leaned forward to see to whom the arm was connected.

It was a girl. I looked her in the eyes, and then I reeled back in horror as the smoke cleared in front of her face. She was a junior at the high school where I taught! Her twin sister stood behind her. I backpedaled down the front steps as the girl smirked at me like she knew I would have taken a pull on the joint.

"We've got to get out of here," I told my friends. "I can't stay here. Let's go. Now."

We hightailed it back to town, and on Monday I knew I'd be face-to-face with the girl again. She gave me a knowing nod as she strolled into my class, coolly indicating that she wouldn't say anything. What she didn't know was that our encounter had only confirmed to me that this town was too small for me to have a social life.

I taught in Hanska for two years and made a total of zero friends. Halfway through my second year, I entertained the idea of moving. Another summer spent working at the print shop to earn extra money and swimming laps at the community pool sounded much less appealing than the thrill of travel. It was time for me to have an adventure, and I'd always wanted to visit California. As soon as school ended in June, I hopped in my yellow Honda Civic hatchback and headed west, detouring a few times to visit family.

Weeks of driving on long, open roads gave me plenty of time to think. I retreated into my head, having conversations with myself about life, spirituality, nature and the world. I had asked Ellie to meet me in California, but she had turned me down. Sad and bummed out, I stewed on my disappointment over the miles. I grew so used to the outward silence that the voices of two people about my age startled me.

I was standing in line on a Friday afternoon at Western Union in San Francisco, waiting for a summer paycheck from my school that my bank in Minnesota was wiring me. It was the first of the month, and the line was long. The two clean-cut, thin, conservatively dressed white college students didn't seem to be waiting in line, but they were friendly, and I welcomed conversation.

"I'm Roy Rogers," the guy said, "and this is Dale Evans." He pointed to the girl next to him. A little weird, but I could hang with their humor.

"Yeah, right," I replied. "And my name's Trigger."

I didn't realize I'd perhaps prophetically named myself after a horse that was already dead, stuffed and on display in a museum.

"We're with the College Association for the Research of Principles," the guy told me. We quickly moved past pleasantries into a conversation about our philosophies of life, culture and business. They were easy to talk to, asking a lot of questions and volunteering very little about themselves.

"You should come have dinner at the center," Roy said. "The food is free, and a lot of people our age go."

California had not panned out like I'd hoped. I was staying at a fraternity house, but the guys spent way more time in class or working summer jobs than partying. I had checked out some of the clubs they recommended, but they weren't that hot. I loved rock and blues, and San Francisco was ushering in the punk scene. An offer of free food and people to talk to sounded great.

I arrived at the center around 3 p.m. and joined in with a few guys throwing a ball around outside. The dinner was surprisingly bland, but I ate it quietly, taking my cues from the others. When they paid rapt attention to a lecturer who gave a talk after dinner, so did I.

"What did you think?" one of the guys asked me after the talk. "If you want to learn more, some of us are going down to this really cool house in L.A. We're leaving in a few minutes."

It was 11 p.m., but I thought, *Why not?* One of the members rode to the frat house with me, where I packed a few things for the weekend. We drove all night, and when I woke up Saturday morning after a few hours' sleep on a strange living room floor, I was surrounded by an unfamiliar group. There wasn't a television, telephone, book, newspaper or magazine in sight.

Whoever they were, these were fun, smart and college-educated people. We ate some granola and fruit for breakfast, then introduced ourselves and told each other how we felt, like something had led us to this place. After a morning lecture, we walked to a park and played soccer. The college students who served as leaders could have moonlighted as high school cheerleaders. Despite little sleep and less to eat, their energy and enthusiasm never waned. In their company, I never felt alone.

I grew up attending church, but I never knew more about God than what I absorbed during the weekly hour-long service. This group seemed to be trying to live a Christian life and make good, moral decisions. They wanted to make the world a better place, and they talked about feeding the hungry and helping other people. As the weekend lectures progressed, I sensed that if we all worked together, we could unify the world. If I stuck with them, I began to believe that I could do some real good. My new friends made me feel so comfortable that I even opened up in one of our sharing sessions, telling them about bad things I had done in my past.

We headed outside on Sunday to throw a football in front of the house, when one of the neighbors walked over to chat with us.

"I'm John," he said. "I heard you guys out here singing. I'm a Christian, too. I actually work at a church around here. What are you up to?"

He seemed genuinely interested in us. Our leaders, however, had no interest in him.

"Okay, everyone!" one guy shouted. "The session's about to start. Back in the house. Let's go!"

We left the neighbor standing on the sidewalk as we dutifully filed inside, not even bothered that we'd rudely walked away from his attempt at a friendly conversation.

❧ ❧ ❧

The weekend turned into three weeks, as the College Association piled into cars and vans on Sunday night for the drive to another house in the San Bernardino Mountains. Somewhere along the way, the leaders had sprung the idea on us that Reverend Sun Myung Moon was actually the Messiah. Even with my limited church exposure, I didn't think a Korean religious leader was the designated savior of the world.

Under normal conditions, I would've rejected the idea, but when you are starved for friendship, physically tired and subsisting on bad food, you tend to go along with the group.

After three weeks in the mountains, absorbing lecture after lecture about Moon's teachings, I called my principal in Minnesota and quit my teaching job. That freed me up for my first assignment in Madison with the Unification Church, as I'd learned my group was officially called.

Using the telephone was tricky. The only phone in our mountain lodge was locked in a room, and to use it another church member had to huddle close to you and listen in on your conversation. My mom had grown accustomed to me calling home every Thursday, but I had missed a few weeks during my stay with the church. When I was finally granted a call home, I quickly explained where I was and that I would be coming through Minnesota on my way to Madison to pick up a few things at my apartment.

"That's the Moonies," I heard my grandmother call out in the background. "You need to get him out of there."

We quickly hung up.

I hadn't fully thrown myself into the Unification Church. I refused to shave my mustache, a common church requirement for new members. The other people had very few things, and I got tired of them wearing my clothes without asking. I insisted on driving my Honda to Madison. They agreed to let me follow the two white vans of church members as long as Eric rode with me, and they allowed me to detour through Minnesota because I offered to share my extensive collection of warm flannel shirts with them. It would be nice to see my parents for a night, but I was looking forward to my work in Madison. Hanging out on college campuses and recruiting people for the church sounded much better than working.

At my parents' house, Eric hardly spoke to us because he was so busy reading every magazine he could find around the place. He seemed to feel the same relief I did at our temporary freedom from the constant lectures about Unification Church philosophies. A good night's sleep and a few meals with protein revived us. In retrospect, there's no surprise that he held on for dear life when my parents' heavies tried to toss him out of the getaway van the next morning.

It took us several days to drive to West Virginia, but I didn't leave the van. My parents supplied me with food and a coffee can, following orders to deliver me straight to the Old Man, a cult-deprogramming expert. As we drove by several similar white vans the police had pulled over, I knew that Eric had been picked up, and the church had notified police that I had been kidnapped. I certainly wouldn't have been the first.

When my minders took over the driving, we flew past the white vans and barreled onto a series of country roads. In my mind, I pictured an old Dracula movie with a stagecoach pulled by spooked horses running crazy through the woods. We screeched to a halt at "The Farm," a cabin with walls built from locally cut stone. It sat alone on several acres, the nearest neighbor miles away. My mind was tangled as I wondered how in three weeks' time I'd quit my job, made a whole new group of friends, been kidnapped by my own parents and taken to a house in West Virginia.

The Old Man opened the doors, and his associate, Miss D, stood behind him. He was short and stout with dark hair formed into a widow's peak accented by gray temples.

I was scared.

"Come in." He ushered me through the door. "Let's have dinner."

We started talking, and our conversations went on for three weeks. With some rest and good food, I came to my senses. I learned that one of the Old Man's helpers had refused a scholarship to study law at Oxford University when he came under the spell of the Moonies.

The Old Man walked me through comparisons between the Unification Church's theology and the Bible.

He'd point to a passage in the Bible. "This is what the Bible says, and this is what they say. Who are you going to believe?"

Even though my background with God had involved nominal church visits and saying a blessing before family meals, I believed in God, not Reverend Moon. I began to understand that in joining the Unification Church, I had made an emotional decision that was manipulated by the people in my surroundings. The Old Man wasn't trying to manipulate me into any particular thoughts about God, but by rebuilding my self-confidence and decision-making skills, I was preparing to make informed decisions about God on my own. Trust had to be earned, though, and I still viewed the church with a large dose of skepticism.

My deprogramming lasted three weeks, during which other recently kidnapped cult members came and went. The Old Man was particularly impressed with how I had talked with a new arrival from The Christ Family, using counseling techniques I'd learned in high school and college. He asked me to join his team of "kidnappers."

I lasted a year and a half, traveling all over the United States and Canada like an undercover agent, snatching people from cults at the request of their parents and delivering them to West Virginia. I took a break, however, when my team flew to California to extract a longtime member of The Way International. I could tell the guy didn't want to go, and I advised my team to abandon the mission. They refused, and I flew back to Minnesota. The man they kidnapped kicked out the back window of the van en route to the Old Man's, and my group was arrested for felony kidnapping when police pulled them over. They went to jail, and the incident put the Old Man out of business.

THE MYSTERIOUS TREE

I needed a new start. Ellie, who I'd kept in touch with, had moved to Houston, so I joined her there. The wide open spaces and roads in Texas would be ideal for riding my motorcycle, which the Old Man had given me at the end of his legal battle because he still owed me part of my salary. I'd ridden bikes in West Virginia, and I couldn't get enough of the thrill of hugging curves at high speeds and the sense of freedom the bike gave me.

Ellie was happy to see me, but her reaction to the motorcycle was lukewarm at best. However, I couldn't shake the thrill of my new hobby. I saved long and hard for my first BMW motorcycle, and it became my weekend companion of choice. I'd hop on the bike on Friday afternoons for a weekend of riding, putting 20,000 miles on the bike the first year I owned it. I hit it off with a few fellow BMW owners I met at a bike rally in West Texas, and we'd get together several times a year to ride in the Hill Country north of San Antonio. Sometimes I'd ride 1,000 miles a weekend, camping when I could. On my first long trip from Houston to Arkansas, I was so invigorated that I tacked on several hundred more miles to visit my grandparents in Iowa.

Out to dinner one night with Ellie to celebrate her birthday, she summed up the situation.

"All you ever talk about is that motorcycle and riding," she said.

"Well, that's all I've been doing."

We struggled on and off for four years before the relationship finally gave its last gasp. By that time,

Meloney, fresh out of prison, had walked into my life.

I ran into work late one day, shoving the last bite of a hamburger in my mouth as I rushed through the door. I'd ridden my motorcycle to the job, and I strode in wearing my leather riding jacket with my helmet tucked under my arm.

A statuesque brunette in a nice dress pushed through the double doors in the back of our building with our other two managers.

"She's here to apply for a job," one of them announced.

I chewed last bits of burger as I measured my irritation against my appreciation for this pretty woman. I wanted to promote someone from the company into the job she was applying for because if an experienced person was working it, I was free to take a promotion. If Meloney was hired, I was stuck training her.

Meloney was not an ideal candidate by any stretch. As I eventually learned, her parents' marriage went through a rough patch when she was 14, and her mother tended to over-share the details of her father's infidelity and ensuing relationship entanglements. Desperate to escape, Meloney started hanging out with older guys who rode Harley motorcycles. She got hooked on morphine, and to support her habit, she became a professional shoplifter.

Her business was similar to that of a personal shopper, except Meloney didn't pay for anything her clients wanted. Her specialty was expensive women's clothing, and she took orders from customers for high-priced items.

Her purse was regularly stuffed with $2,000 or $3,000 in cash. She went to prison three times, and she was labeled a habitual felon the last time because she bit the security guard who caught her and stomped on his foot. She was charged with theft and assault and took a five-year plea deal.

After three years in prison, Meloney decided to turn her life around. She opened a Bible to chapter 8 of the book of Romans, which states, "And we know that in all things God works for the good of those who love him, who have been called according to his purpose." In prison, she went to Alcoholics Anonymous meetings, church services and anything else she could find that would keep her busy. She started praying for the life she wanted, which included a good man and the right job.

The job at my company was the only job that Meloney applied for when she got out of prison and moved into a halfway house. I didn't want to hire her, but she was adamant. She called after her first interview and convinced me to give her a second interview. She quickly won over the other two supervisors, and I agreed to hire her if they would train her.

☙ ☙ ☙

I have always liked live music and dancing, and the Ready Room in Houston was one of the coolest places in town because a lot of touring musicians who lived in Houston made it their neighborhood bar. I'd often round up my coworkers to go out after our shift, and one night, my coworker Joann called Meloney to join us.

We danced to the heavy sounds of the live blues music, so into it — and each other — that at one point the drummer waved a white towel at us indicating that we needed to cool it down. When I went to the bathroom, Meloney stood outside and waited for me.

I enjoyed Meloney's company — she also liked to ride motorcycles — but I wasn't quite detangled emotionally from my relationship with Ellie, even though she was on a trip to Indonesia with another guy.

"We're going to get back together when she comes back," I told Meloney, who seemed unfazed. "We can hang out in the meantime, if you want."

Meloney, a force of nature herself, talked to God a lot. She would tell God about how much she wanted Ellie to come back because Meloney believed that when Ellie showed up, she would go back to her old ways. That way, Meloney figured, I'd see that she was a much better choice. "She doesn't love you the way you need to be loved," Meloney would tell me, her hazel, green-flecked eyes unblinking.

Sure enough, Ellie returned, and we tried to work it out. Within two days, however, our relationship was in shambles, and I was on the phone with Meloney.

"She gone," I told her.

"I'll be right over."

Meloney loved deeply, and she taught me what true love is all about.

THE MYSTERIOUS TREE

కాకాకా

When the printing business slowed down in Houston in the late 1980s, I was laid off from my job. I found another job right away, but it wouldn't start until September, which was three months away. With the summer free, a cross-country trip to Oregon to visit my parents sounded ideal.

Because I was collecting unemployment, I had to stop and apply for jobs along the way during my 10,000-mile motorcycle trip. I started seriously looking for employment in Seattle, but the traffic reminded me too much of Houston. Portland seemed more promising, but a company that interested me there was difficult to get in touch with. As I was closing my hotel room door to check out, I heard the phone ring inside. It was the guy from Wyeast Color, who wanted to talk to me. After a good interview, they offered me the job. Meloney already had planned to fly out later that week, and I agreed to start in October if Meloney found Portland to be a place she could live.

I picked her up at the airport in San Francisco, and as we rode north, she saw the Pacific Ocean for the first time. I don't know if it was God or the Oregon weather, but for the particular week she came to visit, the misty, damp Portland weather gave way to sunny, pleasant days. We were soon packing up in Houston and shipping our things to Oregon. We didn't get married, but we bought a house together in a quiet Portland subdivision and settled down.

ক্রিক্রিক্রি

"MELONEY!"

My head literally was stuck under our Honda Prelude, and my girlfriend seemed to have fallen asleep in a back bedroom of our house.

We had endured a horrible week.

Meloney's brother had died unexpectedly from an overdose of chemotherapy drugs, and we'd flown to Texas for the funeral. When our plane landed in Portland, it was freezing, and our car wouldn't start in the remote parking lot. When a cab dropped us off at our house, we found the water pipes were frozen.

The Prelude was towed to our house, and I jacked it up and figured out that the fuel pump, which is under the rear wheel, was causing the problem. Meloney started the car, while I shimmied under it to see if fuel was coming out of the pump. It wasn't.

Meloney went back inside, emotionally and physically exhausted from the week, to take a nap while I replaced the fuel pump. I pushed and pulled on the pump, trying to wrestle it from the underside of the car.

The vehicle shifted above me, and I pressed up with both hands in a futile effort to keep the 3,000-pound machine from rolling on top of me. I'd forgotten to put blocks behind the rear wheels, and Meloney had left the car in neutral.

The back of the car eased down to the ground, pinning my head in an open space between the rocker panel and the floor. The metal pressed on my jugular, and I could feel the blood rushing through the constricted vein.

God, don't let Meloney walk out here and find me dead. Her brother just died a few days ago. I'm not ready to go.

The stereo was blasting out songs from my six-CD changer, which I'd set on shuffle for a mix of music. It kept choosing my Grateful Dead CD, and the lyric "And I can't tell my pillow from a stone" from the song "Black Muddy River" must have played three times. As my head pressed into the concrete garage floor, the words couldn't have been more appropriate — or more poorly timed.

"MELONEY!" I bellowed, even though I knew there was no way she'd hear me over the music. She'd likely fallen into a deep sleep, anyway.

Yelling was not going to save me. I took a deep breath and contorted my body until I could wedge my feet in the doorframe and lift the car enough that it wasn't crushing my neck. My head was still stuck, though, and I needed help.

With some stretching, I reached my foot to the steering wheel and pressed on the horn. I honked and honked, but no one came.

Thirty minutes, then 45 minutes passed. Meloney and I were scheduled to have dinner with friends, so I knew that at some point they would call, hopefully waking Meloney up.

All I could do was wait and occasionally honk the horn. I started thinking about God and about my life.

ANTHEM

Meloney and I were living together, but I still hadn't married her, despite her mom's not-so-subtle hints that I make her daughter "an honest woman." We liked to go to bars, as Portland had a hopping music scene, and we had never met a beer we didn't like. Marriage was important to Meloney, and her family regularly was asking God to prompt us to get married so that our choices would be in line with what the Bible said about marriage. Perhaps it was time to make some changes.

The most welcome banging noise I'd ever heard startled me from my thoughts.

"Help!" I cried out.

"Willie." I heard my neighbor's voice outside the garage door. "I think they're in trouble."

"What do you want me to do?" Willie yelled through the door. Dottie had heard the honking horn and decided something was wrong. They'd come over to investigate.

"Should I open the garage door?"

"No!" I shouted. The front of the car was wedged against the door, keeping it from further crushing me. "Break down the front door, and come in the garage through the house."

Willie, who is not a big guy, somehow lifted the rear bumper, allowing me to slide out from under the car. I tried to sit up, but I couldn't, really. I lay on the garage floor, trying to catch my breath.

After a visit to the hospital and a few months healing from bruises and badly strained muscles, I recovered. God, however, had gotten my attention.

THE MYSTERIOUS TREE

જીજીજી

It took a few years, but Meloney and I started going to Anthem Church in Portland. We got married and moved into our dream house, complete with a sunroom. Meloney, who had trouble finding jobs because of her felony conviction, had started her own business cleaning houses. She was serious about getting to know God and changing her life, and now this former master shoplifter was the trusted housekeeper for several Portland police officers and the Multnomah County sheriff.

I, too, was turning to God, but I was cautious. I had almost been sucked into the Moonies as a young man, and I didn't want to get caught up in another personality cult. The teachings of our former and current pastors, however, built a solid foundation for my understanding of God and my growing friendship with him. I have always been reserved about spirituality and skeptical about people's claims about God. These pastors were always careful to draw parallels between their teaching and the Bible, always backing up what they had to say with verses from the Bible.

Words used a lot in church, such as salvation and restoration, began to make more sense to me. I understood that God wanted to get to know me, and because I was a fallible person who had made many mistakes, I needed a real Messiah, someone with true spiritual power who could offer me forgiveness for my errors.

In 1997, my life turned around the day I acknowledged to God that I was not in control and that, with God's guidance, I could make better choices. Thanks to our pastor's sermons, I learned that the Bible is a trustworthy guidebook for life, and if I got serious about reading it and talking with God by praying, I would have a stronger faith and a different kind of life. I started praying at random times of the day and making sure that my actions reflected what I believed.

God provided the ideal place for me to quietly grow in my faith. My wife and I were offered the chance to be caretakers of a home that sits on 40 acres on top of a mountain, and it was beautiful. We liked to walk our dog along the snow-covered road, and talking to God was easy in the quiet of the wintry outdoors. Meloney, who loved to pray, would spend an hour a day talking to God while staring out the window at a tree shaped like a perfect Christmas tree growing amid hundreds of raspberry bushes.

While there were days, too, that I didn't pray or wake up thankful for things in my life, I began to understand the value of a long-term commitment to knowing God better. I saw that as we poured our lives and resources into building a friendship with God and supporting our church, God looked out for us. He provided for our needs over and over in the most extraordinary ways.

THE MYSTERIOUS TREE

While Meloney was involved in a lot of questionable activities in her youth, she never smoked. In 2007, she developed a cough that wouldn't go away. She made an appointment with our family practitioner to get some antibiotics, and she insisted on having a chest X-ray while she was in the office to see what was going on.

The scan showed a little spot on one of her lungs, but the doctor said it could be scaring from pneumonia. He wanted to keep an eye on it, so Meloney made an appointment to return in six months. The cough went away, but when she came back to the doctor, the spot had grown a little.

She went back in for a CAT scan.

The doctor didn't have good news. "You have lung cancer, and we need to do a biopsy," he told us, his face grim. "It appears to be inoperable."

We learned that the symptoms of lung cancer often don't show up until the disease has significantly progressed, and Meloney's was already at stage 3. The doctor laid out options for chemotherapy and radiation, telling Meloney the treatment may make her very sick but that she could survive this cancer.

However, we weren't ready to accept the doctor's bleak outlook for Meloney's treatment. We walked out of his office shell-shocked, wondering how this news could possibly be true.

"This is wrong," we told each other. "We won't accept this negative report." We prayed that Jesus would heal Meloney.

105

Two or three weeks went by. We both were getting over a bad case of the flu, and Meloney kept putting the doctor off when he called, telling her she needed to get started on her treatment. Finally, she fired him and went to another doctor.

The new doctor ran blood tests. The results showed no cancer markers, which the doctor said are always present when a patient has lung cancer.

"See," Meloney told him. "Leaders in my church prayed for me, and I'm healed."

But while the blood work may have come back clean, the cancer wasn't gone. Meloney was wary of chemotherapy because of her brother's experience, so with her doctor's blessing, she headed to Amarillo, Texas, her hometown, for naturopathic treatment. She stayed for three months at a cost of $15,000. Her doctor in Portland said the treatment was working, but we couldn't afford to continue on that path. He reiterated that chemotherapy and radiation would give her the best shot at survival.

After a round of treatment, Meloney took another trip to Texas that turned out to be her last. Further chemotherapy wasn't working, so the doctor helped her get into a study for an experimental drug; Meloney wasn't going to go without a fight.

Even though God hadn't healed Meloney, we didn't lose faith. God never abandoned us. In fact, he provided for us in ways we didn't expect. When we couldn't afford to fly to California twice a month for her experimental treatments, a pilot friend provided vouchers for flights.

People stepped up to help as we began selling our possessions to pay for treatment.

Ironically, Meloney's pain became so unbearable that she was put on morphine, the drug that led her to shoplifting as a teenager. Breathing became difficult.

On the day Meloney decided to stay home from church because she was tired, I tried to rouse her at 3 p.m.

"I think we need to go to the hospital," she whispered. "I'm having a really hard time breathing today."

We knew the routine and packed the bags like we'd packed them several times before for Meloney's hospital stays. Thirty minutes later, her tone became more urgent.

"Maybe you should call an ambulance."

As the first responders arrived, Meloney looked me in the eye before she got out of her chair and onto the gurney.

"Either way," she said, "I'm going to be fine. I'm just worried about you guys."

With that, we put her on the stretcher and loaded her into the ambulance. At the hospital, nurses put a big mask over her face that forced oxygen into her lungs. Meloney wanted to go to the nearby hospital where she had received treatments, and after she was stabilized, the hospital staff began making arrangements for her transfer.

"I'm going to go outside and make some phone calls," I told her.

She pulled the mask off of her face. "Make sure that you go and thank the paramedics and the ambulance driver."

That was the last conversation I had with my wife. After about a week without improvement, we decided to take her off the ventilator and increase her medication to keep her comfortable until the end.

The week before she died, Meloney ironed every shirt in my closet. She had always put me before herself, and if I asked her to do something a particular way, she made the effort to at least consider my request.

One Christmas when money was tight and we had agreed to spending limits on presents, she used money she had stashed away to buy me a leather jacket she knew I wanted. I cried that Christmas morning.

When I found that closet full of neatly pressed shirts during her final week in the hospital, I knew she had done it because deep down she understood she wouldn't be there to take care of me anymore. In the weeks after her death, it would have been so easy to slip into the bitter loneliness that had gripped my life years before. But somehow, God kept me going. He was with me, making sure I was never really alone.

❧❧❧

Every year, Meloney and I had attended the Waterfront Blues Festival in Portland with the same group of friends. The year before she was diagnosed, we heard Paul Thorn, whose music reflected the unusual influences of his father, who was a Pentecostal preacher, and his uncle, who was a pimp. During one of his songs, the huge crowd gathered in front of the stage, pressing toward Paul and his band.

"Raise your hands," he called out, singing the song's chorus.

> Glory Hallelujah
> Thank you, Jesus
> Praise the Lord
> I'm still here

Amazingly, the crowd responded, singing along and waving their arms in the air.

My friends and I looked at each other and laughed when it was all over. Portland is possibly the least religious city in America.

"Did we just have church?"

About six months before Meloney died, we read that Paul Thorn would be playing at the upcoming BMW Motorcycle Owner Association International Rally in Redmond, Oregon. That was close to us, and we were excited that we'd be able to go. But as the date got closer, our plans changed from taking the car instead of the motorcycle to only driving over for the show to not going at all. She died on July 5, and two weeks later was the date of the rally. Her parents encouraged me to go. We decided that's what Meloney would have wanted, too.

More than 4,000 people attended the rally, arriving on more than 3,000 motorcycles. I took off by myself, and as I pulled into the rally site, I heard someone call my name.

"Larry?" It was one of my good friends from church who rides a Honda. "What are you doing at the BMW rally?"

A guy who rides BMWs had asked him to come along. Was this a coincidence? I think it was God's provision once again, sending a friend when I most needed one. Larry didn't shy away from the topic of Meloney, reminding me of how funny she was and that she wouldn't want me sitting alone feeling sorry for myself. Of course times had been better, Larry told me, but better times were to come, which Meloney was already experiencing. She was now living forever with God.

As I passed through the registration line, I heard my name again. "Is that Mike Bates?" a woman drawled in a thick Texas accent. There stood two women from our BMW club in Houston.

My emotions were raw, and it was good to have friends to talk to that night. At the Paul Thorn concert, I sat by myself in the back, where it was dark. I had a few laughs — Paul is from Mississippi and tells great stories in a great Southern accent — and I had a good cry.

Attending Paul Thorn concerts became a meaningful way for me to acknowledge the anniversary of Meloney's death and celebrate her life. In 2011, however, Paul's show at the BMW rally would be held across the country in Pennsylvania. Always up for an adventure, I made arrangements to fly to Brunswick, New York, buy a bike there and ride home after the concert.

The bike ran great. After stops in Indiana, Iowa,

Wyoming and Montana, I camped my last night in Kooskia, Idaho. The place was packed because of a local festival, but a bed and breakfast owner let me camp in her backyard by her chicken coop. I stayed up late talking to festival goers and woke up with the rooster at 5:30 a.m.

I could only find one teabag in the kitchen for my morning drink — I preferred two — so I hit the road a little light on my daily caffeine. An hour down the road, I passed a coffee shop advertising cinnamon rolls. I ignored the voice in my head telling me to turn back and get one. *Besides,* I reasoned to myself, *it's only 20 miles to the next stop.* The sun was finally warming the air, and I knew if I could just get to Walla Walla, I could get gas, use the bathroom and finally get my caffeine, all in one stop. I settled into the straight highway through rolling hills of tan wheat. I checked my speedometer, which registered about 60 miles per hour.

With no forewarning, no head bobbing, no heavy eyelids, I dropped into a deep sleep.

The impact of the bike on the low, loose gravel shoulder of the road jolted me awake. The small rocks flew out from under my front wheel as I plowed through the gravel much too fast. The lip back onto the road was too high to manage at 60 miles per hour, so I let the bike drift to the right toward a ditch.

Okay. The bike is slowing down. I can save this.

I hit a patch of high weeds and then the only boulder authorities later could find anywhere near me. My left engine guard caught the rock. The bike stopped, and I felt myself launch over the handlebars and into the air, like a stone from a slingshot.

My knees and side hurt. I opened my eyes and looked around. I slowly moved my fingers and toes, all of which seemed to work. I gingerly turned my head side to side, then opened my face shield and spit a few rocks out of my mouth.

Glory hallelujah. Thank you, Jesus. Praise the Lord. I'm still here.

"Are you okay?" a voice came from above.

"No."

"You want me to take that helmet off for you?" The stranger unstrapped my helmet and pulled it off, then pulled my duffle bag out of the ditch for me to lay my head on.

"I was working in my yard and heard this strange sound," the man recounted. "I walked up to the road and saw a big cloud of dust. Some ladies coming from the other direction saw you go off the road and called 911."

Within three minutes, fire trucks, EMTs and even the sheriff had arrived. They loaded me in the ambulance, and we were off to the hospital. X-rays showed cracked ribs and a broken leg, and when I tried to put weight on my left foot, the pain was so intense that I passed out.

෴

I had to figure out how to get home. Who should I call? Portland was about 250 miles away, and my bike had already been deposited in a local wrecking yard, not that I could ride it home in my condition, anyway. I settled on my friend Donny, a fellow church member and motorcycle rider.

Donny was at a carwash raising money to help young girls caught in prostitution, but he offered to end the event right then and come get me. I breathed a sigh of relief. Someone was coming.

We drove into Portland around 1 a.m., and thankfully my keys had been salvaged from the wreck, and I could open the door to my house.

"What can I do to help you?" Donny asked. "What do you need?"

I surveyed the living room. If we moved some furniture around, I could sleep in my recliner. Donny helped me settle in, and I drifted off for some much-needed sleep.

My immediate problem the next day was how to get myself around. I lived alone, and I needed a wheelchair. I needed to shower.

My friends Frank and Mel helped me into the shower, where I sat under the hot water in Meloney's shower chair for a long time, washing off the dirt and gravel that seemed embedded in my skin. When I turned off the water, I could hear voices outside.

"Hey!" I called out to Frank and Mel. "What's going on?"

"Your neighbors are building you a ramp."

My motorcycle crash taught me, more than anything,

that God had provided the kind of real friends I had always longed for. Not the kind who were too busy when you really needed help, but the kind who drive you to doctors' appointments, bring you dinner and help you take care of your dog when you can't get around.

On Saturdays, I would roll my wheelchair down the ramp to soak up some sun in my driveway, and my neighbor Kyle would walk over and hang out for a few hours.

Still, living by myself had its lonely moments. After several weeks, I moved from the wheelchair to crutches and then to my own two feet. I was ambulatory, but I knew I was spending too much time by myself.

I met Pastor Brad and his wife, Lisa, in the church parking lot one Tuesday night as I was going into the church to teach a class.

"You should meet me next Tuesday at Buffalo Wild Wings, and we'll have dinner," I called out.

"You know," Pastor Brad suggested over a meal a week later, "this would be a great place to have a small group. You should get some guys together and start meeting at Buffalo Wild Wings."

That's what I did. I rounded up some guys from my church, including Frank and my friend Mel, and we met there every week. Then I organized a men's breakfast and a men's retreat. Soon, I was the leader of ministries for men at my church.

When I used to go out with Meloney, total strangers regularly would walk up to her and talk, telling her all sorts of things. There was an openness about her that drew people to her.

As I spent more time reading the Bible, praying and hanging out with other people, I noticed that I seemed to suddenly have Meloney's affect. People I crossed paths with now were talking to *me*, sharing bits and pieces of their lives. More than once, I had the opportunity to pray about their situations, invite them to Anthem and offer words of encouragement.

You can do a lot on your own. But not everything. I'm still climbing out of the valley of loss and loneliness, but I know now that if the phone doesn't ring, it might be a sign that I need to pick it up and call someone myself. I've learned that everyone needs family, and I've found mine in the people of Anthem.

❧❧❧

A month before Meloney died, we made a trip to California for her experimental cancer treatment.

I woke up at 4 a.m. one morning convinced that I needed to drive to Long Beach and visit West Coast Choppers. Maybe we could even see the owner, Jesse James.

Meloney was game for this crazy pursuit, so we drove 40 miles to Long Beach and pulled up in front of West Coast Choppers, his now-defunct custom motorcycle shop. It was dark inside, but I could see shadows of people working in the back.

I knew that Jesse James had opened a restaurant around the corner, so we walked over. Who walked out with a bowl of food but Jesse James himself. I introduced myself and then Meloney, who was rail thin from chemotherapy and whose hair was now short and gray.

On the way back to the car, we stopped in front of the gate to the workshop where we noticed Jessie had fashioned a stainless steel Maltese cross. Its smooth silver surface reflected the sky.

Meloney took my picture under the cross, and then I took hers. Four days later, I downloaded the images onto my computer.

I did a double take when I saw Meloney's picture. The two photos were taken moments apart and from the same angle, and there were no trees facing the cross. However, in the center of the cross *only* in Meloney's picture there is a distinct, detailed tree, with two long branches extending to the sides like a cross.

It's a sign that her life is in balance, I mused. *God is the trunk, the center, supporting the tilting scale of her life. Maybe the right branch represents her crazy days and prison life, and the left branch depicts her life of knowing God. The brushy top could be all of the lives she's touched.*

I'm always one to approach supposed signs with skepticism, but I believe this was from God. Since Meloney passed away, the picture has held an even deeper meaning to me. The image is too clear, too deliberate, for it to be anything else.

I keep the photo on my iPad. I've shown it to people around the country on my travels, including the guy at Buck Lake Ranch in Indiana and friends and acquaintances, both Christian and non-Christian. I've found that people who have a relationship with God have an immediate reaction to it.

Meloney is gone, and there are lots of things I still don't understand. I don't consider myself a religious man, but I am a man of faith. All I know is that God has made himself known to me and has given me an authentic, caring extended family. He reminds me that he is with me all of the time, a comforter and a best friend. I know now that God provides the lonely with true friends and a future filled with hope. The day my parents kidnapped me and saved me from a cult, I believed I was in control of my own destiny. Now, I've learned that God truly is the great orchestrator of it all.

MUSIC FOR MY SOUL
The Story of Hannah Partridge
Written by Karen Koczwara

He was going to kill me.

Right there on the floor of his apartment, Mario was going to pull the trigger and take my life.

My pulse raced so rapidly I was sure he could see it in my throbbing veins as he pressed the gun to my neck. My insides were a tornado, but I trained my gaze straight ahead to meet his cold, calculating glare.

"You're not going to call the cops, are you?" he demanded.

"No," I replied robotically.

Just stay calm, Hannah.

"And you're not going to take my son away from me, are you?"

Again, I uttered a "no." The tornado was now a hurricane, thrashing around inside me while I clenched my trembling hands to my side. My toddler son wailed nearby, terrified.

Somehow, I had known deep down it might come to this. Somehow, I had known he might try to kill me.

Be brave, Hannah. Tell him what he wants. It's your only hope of staying alive …

I was born in Portland, Oregon, on December 6, 1983, two years behind my older brother. My mother suffered two miscarriages after I was born, and the doctors told her she would never have any more children. But when I was 5, my mother gave birth to another little girl. She focused on caring for three kids and working part time as a nutritional expert at an herbal shop. My father worked full time as a mechanical engineer for a refrigeration company. Our busy little family seemed complete.

We'd moved to a two-story home in Gresham, just outside Portland, when I was 2. Situated on a corner lot, the house offered plenty of room inside and outside to play. A huge walnut tree out front provided ample shade and long, thick branches perfect for climbing. I was a bit of a tomboy; mud-covered knees at the end of the day meant I'd had an afternoon of delightful fun. And when the sun went down, I curled up in bed with a good book and read until my eyes drooped and sleep called.

My parents took us to church each Sunday and homeschooled us. While they did everything to make our home a happy and safe place, my innocence was clouded at an early age when I was sexually abused. A childhood family friend, just a year older than me, invited me into her little playhouse out back. What seemed like an innocent afternoon of fun quickly turned into a strange, manipulative game.

"This is all your fault," she whispered after she'd touched me in places I knew were wrong. "And you better not tell anyone, you hear me?"

I nodded solemnly and promised that I'd never tell. But the terrible knot in my stomach grew a little bit bigger, for I knew something was not right.

I began taking piano lessons when I was 6. I loved the music that filled the air as my little fingers glided over the black and white keys. The knot in my stomach disappeared when I played, replaced by a contentment in my soul. I had a hunch that music would play a very big part in my life as I got older.

My childhood friend continued to sexually abuse me for the next five years. I was too young to fully comprehend her actions, but I knew it made me uncomfortable and felt very wrong. Still, because our families were friends and I did not want to upset anyone, I kept the secret to myself and put on a smile for the world.

When I was 10, my mother learned she was pregnant. The news came as a surprise to all of us, as she'd been so sure she'd never give birth again. We welcomed another baby into our home, a little boy named Peter. I loved my brother dearly, but his arrival was soon followed by serious worries about my mother's health, which took a turn for the worse. Doctors scratched their heads as they sought to treat her mysterious condition. Her nervous system shut down, and she described the shooting pains that radiated through her body as "lightning bolts." Unable to eat much due to the pain, she grew extremely weak and fatigued, and her medication made her agitated and angry.

"Hannah! Get in here right now! I told you to feed that

baby an hour ago!" my mother screamed at me one afternoon.

"I'm sorry. I was just working on homework." I sighed, picked up little Peter and made him a bottle. Inwardly, I grew resentful of my new duties and wished I could just go back to being an average, carefree 10-year-old little girl. I wanted my life — and my mother — back.

The peacefulness in our home turned to tension. My father came home every night, weary from a long day's work. He retreated to his room, while I continued to care for the baby. My mother's anger worsened, and my temper rose as well. After two years of watching my mother struggle, I was relieved when she discovered some helpful herbal remedies and finally began to get better. I hoped we could embrace a sense of normalcy again and go on with life.

When I was 12 years old, just on the cusp of adolescence, another friend invited me to sleep over at her house. She quickly grew aggressive after we went to bed and sexually abused me. Something inside of me shut down at that moment, and I locked the memory deep inside, along with my emotions. It would be years before I'd find the key to unlock it again.

To the world, I was a happy, well-adjusted homeschooled teenage girl. I took extracurricular classes, enjoyed literature and drama and continued playing the piano. In 1994, I began working with the youth at our church, playing the piano and singing with elementary school-aged kids. I loved being at church. It was a refuge, a happy place where I was loved and could love others.

But a deep pain sank into my heart, a bleeding gash I could not fix. I did not know where the pain came from; I only knew that I hurt. I lashed out at my friends and family in anger and often fled to my room, where I hid from the world and buried myself in a book. And sometimes, when I felt like the pain might explode from within, I sat at the piano and played sad songs for hours. Music was more than an outlet — it was the gauze for my wounds.

In 2002, I graduated from high school and went on to Bible college. I threw myself into my studies and eagerly attended several mission conferences, where I learned how others were sharing God's love around the world. The medical field sounded intriguing; perhaps nursing was the way to go. But within a few weeks of beginning classes, my health began to take a turn for the worse. I woke up with excruciating chest pains that plagued me throughout the day. At last, I went to the doctor for help.

"The good news is, there's nothing serious going on, and your heart looks fine," the doctor reported after running some tests. "It appears you have some sort of inflammation in your chest cavity, which I believe is a condition called costochondritis. It usually occurs after trauma, like a severe car accident or something. But since you haven't been in an accident, I'm not quite sure why your pain is so bad. At this point, we'll just keep an eye on it and try to keep the pain under control."

I began classes at Mt. Hood Community College in

2004, where I debated what to study as a major. The opportunity arose to work at an orphanage in Mexico for three months the following summer. I prayed and submitted an application online. A few weeks later, I was on a plane headed south. I enjoyed every moment of my time at the orphanage, where I worked with nearly 50 kids on the site. I had a passion for children and felt I was meant to spend my life working with them in some capacity. But a nagging depression clouded my joy everywhere I went, and I didn't know how to erase it.

I returned to Mt. Hood that fall and finished out my classes there. In 2006, I began attending George Fox University, turning my major to psychology. Toward the end of my spring term, I met a handsome Hispanic guy named Mario at the restaurant where I worked. Short, broad-shouldered, with dark eyes and a huge smile, Mario was funny, charming and sweet. While other guys seemed to view me as just an ordinary girl, Mario saw something special in me and had the ability to make me feel like a princess. By summertime, we were dating.

One evening, Mario pulled me in for a kiss. As his lips brushed against mine, something inside of me froze. Though I had dated a few guys in the past, I had always shied away from physical contact. I had known the inevitable moment might come, but I was not prepared for the reaction that followed.

"What's wrong?" Mario asked, his dark eyes searching mine as he pulled away.

"Nothing," I stammered, trying to smile. "I'm fine."

Inside, a horrible, familiar knot formed in my stomach, and my heart began to race. I gently backed off and told him I needed to head home.

That night, as I lay in my dorm room bed, the horrible memories of my childhood trauma returned in a flood. I had tried for years to repress them, but the instant Mario kissed me, I suddenly remembered it all. Finally, it all made sense — the sadness that followed me wherever I went, the anger that overwhelmed me for no reason, the mysterious chest pain. Was it all due to the trauma?

I grew angry as my mind took me back to those dark nights as a little girl. *Why, God?* I railed. *Why would you let that happen to me? I was too young to fight back! All these years, I've been living a huge lie. Everyone thinks I'm the perfect Christian girl, but I'm not. I'm tainted, ruined. My life is a mess!*

As each memory came back, it was as if those horrible things had just occurred the day before. When nighttime fell, I thrashed in my bed, tormented by nightmares, waking up in a sweat, my heart thudding in my chest. I had never felt so alone and terrified in all my life.

One day, during a team-building exercise on campus, I suddenly panicked as my peers closed in around me. I let out a scream and pushed everyone to the side. "Get away from me!" I cried. I escaped the circle and ran off, enveloped by another wave of terror. What was happening to me?!

Unable to talk to anyone about what I was going through, I closed myself off from the world and focused on my studies. One day, I learned that the university offered counseling, and I decided to give it a try. I was at my wit's end, and perhaps a safe place to discuss things would be a good start.

The director of the counseling program offered to see me himself. I sat across from him in my chair during our visit, wringing my hands, sweating and wondering if I should have come.

"What brings you here, Hannah?" he asked kindly.

Slowly, tearfully, it all tumbled out. I shared how I had been sexually abused as a child and repressed it for years until a physical incident triggered it all.

"I think you're experiencing post traumatic stress syndrome," the counselor began. "I know this is going to be painful, but we're going to go back in your mind and walk through every one of those details, okay? This will help in the healing process."

I nodded, but inside, I still felt sick to my stomach. I'd heard about people experiencing physical symptoms after traumatic incidents in their past. Perhaps this syndrome explained my mysterious physical conditions as well.

Over the course of the next four months, we walked through all the memories together. Each detail felt like a slap to the face or a knife to my back. The counselor encouraged me to continue the process, saying that we could not move forward until we went back. I was grateful for someone to finally talk to after keeping the terrible secret to myself all those years, but I wished I could just snap my fingers and make the pain go away for good.

Despite the counseling, I grew angrier with God. *I'm done with you*, I raged at God one day. *I tried my whole life to be a good kid, but you abandoned me when I needed you most. I've been holding on to doing the right thing all these years, but I'm done. I'm going to do whatever I want.*

I continued dating Mario, and we began sleeping together. Mario sensed that something was wrong with me and pressed me to talk about it.

"I'm fine. I really don't want to talk," I insisted. Instead, I pulled him toward me for a kiss. Now that I was no longer a good girl, what did it matter if I slept with him or anyone else?

My health problems returned with a vengeance. Pain radiated throughout my entire body, but my hips bothered me most of all. Severe headaches plagued me, and I had trouble keeping my food down. Some days, it was all I could do to get out of bed and tie my shoes. I returned to the doctor, and he told me they'd originally misdiagnosed me. I didn't have costochondritis — I had an autoimmune disease, lupus. It was not life threatening, but it was something I might struggle with for the rest of my life.

A short time after, the doctors changed the diagnosis to fibromyalgia, another mysterious condition that causes chronic muscle pain. I was relieved to finally have answers. But just as that news sank in, I discovered something shocking — I was pregnant!

My mind raced as I considered my options. The school semester was over in a month; I was at the end of my senior year, with my entire life ahead of me. I wasn't ready for a baby, especially in my current physical and emotional condition. What was I going to do?

As I listened to my classmates discuss the latest weekend events and their plans for summer vacation, I felt more alone than ever. My hands drifted to my belly, where inside, life was already formed. I confided in Mario and my roommate but kept my pregnancy secret from the rest of my peers. I went to the doctor for a checkup when I was three months along and learned that I had miscarried.

"There's no heartbeat," the doctor said grimly. "I'm sorry."

I was filled with a wave of emotions. The idea of being pregnant had terrified me, but the idea of losing a child I had yet to meet was just as devastating. I went home and tried to go on with life, but my secret haunted me. It seemed my whole life had been full of secrets while I paraded around with a smile on my face. I was growing weary of keeping up the facade, though; something was bound to crack soon.

Semester finals, papers and deadlines loomed. I went through the motions, cramming for my exams and furiously typing up papers. When classes were over, I packed up my things and moved back home with my parents in Portland. I felt dead inside; the happy girl that had once played piano for children and laughed and sang along with her church friends felt like someone else. I was angry with the world — my parents, my friends and everyone else who had gone on with their lives while I'd experienced painful abuse. Where had they been during my darkest moments? Where had God been? Counseling had helped me address my grief, but it had not given me all the answers to move forward.

I moved in with my brother and decided to party hard to escape from my emotions. Four to five nights a week, I hit the bars, where I drank until I stumbled home in a daze. I had a couple one-night stands as well; if I was choosing to throw my life away, what did it matter how I behaved anymore? Inside, I was cold and lifeless, a shell of the girl I once knew.

"Hannah, you comin' out with us tonight?" one of my new friends asked when she called one afternoon.

"Yeah. Meet you downtown later?" As I hung up the phone, I glanced around my messy bedroom and wondered what I'd wear tonight. I thought of my friends' faces — heads thrown back in stupid laughter after drinking too much. Did it really matter what I wore when we'd all be wasted in a few hours?

I decided to rekindle my relationship with Mario. We had been off and on since first getting together, but something had always drawn me back to him. In my place of loneliness, he was a face of familiarity. In the fall of 2007, I began working at a rehab center for young girls who'd been in jail. As I stared into their weary faces and listened to their sad stories, I suddenly realized that I wasn't doing much better than them. If I kept up my ways, I could easily find myself in their shoes.

I hated who I'd become. When I splashed cold water

on my face and glanced in the mirror in the morning, I hardly recognized the hollow-eyed girl staring back at me. *What are you doing, Hannah?* I chided myself. *Is this the kind of person you really want to be?*

As the weeks passed, I realized something simple but profound: I missed God. I missed my relationship with him, the way I'd once played my heart out for him on the piano and sung songs of praise. I missed talking to him, for he'd once been my best friend. I had never felt more peace than when I was resting in him, trusting him for my daily needs, pouring out my thoughts to him and reading my Bible. Deep in my heart, I took comfort in knowing that, despite the craziness of the world, someone in heaven loved me. I was his child, and though I had been angry at him, I had never truly forgotten him. And I was hopeful that he had not forgotten me, either.

To my surprise, Mario encouraged me to go back to church. "You used to love it so much, Hannah," he reminded me. "Maybe you should give it another chance."

I mulled it over. Maybe he was right. Not only did I miss God, but I missed church, a place where people cared for me and looked forward to seeing me on Sunday mornings. Unlike my partying friends, they took a genuine interest in my life. Was it time to take that next step and go back?

In April 2008, my mother called to invite me to a prayer meeting at her church. I decided to go. The minute I stepped into the building, I knew I was about to encounter something powerful. As people began to pray, tears streamed down my cheeks, and I could not hold them back. My tears turned into heavy sobs, and I knelt there on the floor for the next hour, overwhelmed by emotion. I felt God's presence in that moment, like a thick, warm blanket around my shoulders, comforting me and reminding me that I was just where he wanted me to be. I had come home.

I had fallen in love with Jesus at a young age, when I'd invited him into my life as my Savior and my friend. As a little girl, I'd listened intently as the pastor explained that, though we'd all done wrong things in our life, God had sent his son, Jesus, to earth to settle the score. He'd paid the price for those wrong things when he died a gruesome death on the cross. The wonderful news was that, because of his great love for us, we could spend eternity with him in heaven if we invited him into our hearts and lives.

As a child, things had been so simple. But I had shut down. My joy and peace had been clouded by years of pain that overcame me physically, spiritually and emotionally. When I confronted the memories at last, the pain was unbearable, and I tried to ease it with temporary fixes like partying and relationships. But the only thing I truly needed — Jesus' love — had been right in front of me all along. Even in my deepest pit, I had not been too far from rescuing. And even when hope had seemed unfathomable, Jesus had not let go of me.

My entire body felt lighter when I went home that night. I was excited to be reunited with God, my best friend. I didn't have the rest of life's answers all figured out, but I did know that there had been a real shift in my heart — a release of the pain that had suffocated me for so long. I was free to live, love and laugh again. It was the best feeling I'd experienced in a very long time.

"I think we need to break up," I told Mario the next day. "I really want to get my life back on track, and I believe it's best if we spend time apart." I cared deeply for Mario, but I knew he was not right for me. If I wanted to move forward with my life, I could not do it with him in it.

A few days later, I went to the doctor for a checkup. My health had been better lately, but I still had bouts of pain. As I drove home, I began to calculate when I'd had my last period. Suddenly, dread filled my insides as I realized I was late. I drove to the store, bought a digital pregnancy test and took it as soon as I got home. The minute the word "pregnant" showed up on the little white stick, my heart sank to my toes. I stared at the word over and over, trying to absorb the reality.

God, how could this be happening to me right now? I just turned my life around, and now I'm pregnant? Why now? The tears came again as fear overwhelmed me. I'd just told Mario I didn't want to be with him; how could I now go back and tell him he was going to be the father of my child?

I decided to write my parents a letter, confessing my pregnancy. "I'm so very sorry," I wrote, tears pricking my eyes as I tried to muster the words to tell them the shocking news. "I understand if you are angry with me." I left it at the house and waited nervously for their response.

"Hannah! What are you going to do? How can you be pregnant?" my mother cried when she read the letter.

"I'm sorry. I know, I'm freaking out, too," I cried. "I don't know what to do!"

My parents had been struggling in their marriage and had even talked of separating. I knew my news was especially untimely. Surely, God would have answers for us. Surely, he would not leave me hanging after all I'd been through.

I moved in with my old college roommate, who was now married and pregnant. She agreed to charge me only $200 per month for a room, and I was grateful for her help. Even that little amount of money would be a stretch, but with God's help, I would find a way to pay my bills. I continued to work at the treatment center and also part time at the restaurant where Mario and I had met. And each time the money trickled in, I thanked God for his provision.

On January 28, 2009, I gave birth to a little boy named Dominic. Though I was elated at his arrival, the first few days proved especially difficult. Dominic had severe colic and coughed, sputtered and cried each time I tried to breastfeed him. Each feeding session took more than an hour, and I grew weary and frustrated. As his weight declined, I became worried, and so did the doctors.

"We need to transfer him to another children's hospital, where they can assess why he's not thriving," the doctors told me.

I was a young, new single mother and terrified that

something was severely wrong with my baby. We moved Dominic to another hospital, where further evaluation led to the conclusion that he had a swallowing and digestive disorder that made it difficult to eat. He also had a heart defect that was not life threatening but still worrisome. The information was overwhelming. I had no experience with any of this, and the terms sounded scary as the doctors threw them around.

"Dominic is going to require a little extra TLC growing up," one doctor explained. "But he's going to be okay."

The next few months were a blur. Dominic cried all the time. I got little to no sleep and became physically and emotionally exhausted. On the weekends, I went home, and my mother cared for Dominic while I caught up on my sleep. I waded through each day like I had bricks on my feet. Life felt extra hard. I considered going back to church but was too ashamed to do so. I continued to wrestle with God, wondering if I was experiencing such difficulty because of the bad choices I'd made in my life. Maybe it was too late for me to ever really get back on track.

I got a job as a nanny, something I could do while caring for little Dominic. I also decided to start attending Anthem Church with my family. I felt like all eyes were on me as I walked into the church building, my infant son in tow. But to my surprise, people were warm and welcoming, and the walls I'd built around my heart began to slowly crumble.

When my roommate's husband got into trouble with

the law, she was forced to move out of her apartment. Suddenly left with no place to stay, I moved in with my mother. After months of constant fighting, my parents had finally separated. I was devastated by their decision. It seemed that what was left of our perfect little Christian family had now crumbled. The days of homeschooling, church camps and laughter filling the halls were replaced with tears and troubles. Would things ever go back to normal again?

"I hope your father and I can work things out, I really do," my mother told me sadly. "But in the meantime, please know this separation is for the best."

A few people at the church came forward to ask me if I'd like to play the piano for worship.

"Thanks for the offer, but I don't think I'm up for that right now," I declined politely.

I focused on working and caring for Dominic, who continued to be plagued by his health problems. But as I began to pray, something stirred in my heart. I thought back to the wonderful days when I'd played for the children at church. There was something about sitting at the piano, my fingers dancing over the keys as I sang and poured my heart out to God. I had never felt closer to him than in those moments. Perhaps playing for church was exactly what I needed to do right now.

In February 2010, I mustered the courage to join the worship team at Anthem. The first time I sat at the piano on stage and sang out to God, that wonderful warm feeling of peace returned to my heart. As I glanced out at the members of the church, singing along and smiling up at me, I realized I was exactly where God wanted me to be. Life was still uncertain in many ways, but I had found hope again.

In March, my parents reconciled and moved back in together. They bought a new house and asked me if I'd like to move into the basement, which they could turn into an apartment for Dominic and me. I agreed to move in. Meanwhile, I continued to let Mario see Dominic on a regular basis. He was a wonderful father, and though I wanted to believe in my heart that we could make things work between us someday, I wasn't sure we could.

In April, the worship center at the church burned down, and everything was abruptly thrown into disarray. The lead worship pastor stepped down, and suddenly there was a need.

"You should take the position," my new friends encouraged me. "You'd be such a wonderful worship leader."

"Me?" I squeaked. I hardly felt worthy to lead a church in worship. But I told them I'd pray about it, and as I did, I felt God was prompting me in my heart to say yes.

Taking the position was a step of faith, an act of trusting that God would equip me when I did not feel equipped. But I also knew I loved music with every fiber of my being, and if God wanted me to do this, I would obey him.

I accepted the position, and I loved every minute of my new experience. Each Sunday, as the music filled the room, I felt as if Jesus himself was sitting amongst us, singing along with a smile on his face. *Thank you, God,* I prayed. *You've entrusted me, a girl with a painful past, to this amazing position. Help me to pour my whole heart into what I'm doing so that others see you shine through me.*

In July, I decided to take the kids I was nannying for to my parents' house outside the city. With three wooded acres, they'd have plenty of room for an afternoon of outdoor fun with my siblings and family.

"How'd you guys like to roast marshmallows and hot dogs?" I asked the kids as the sun began to go down.

"Yeah!" they screamed in delight.

We gathered a bunch of branches from a tree my parents had just chopped down for a bonfire.

"Here, we can use this gasoline can," my younger brother suggested, coming outside.

"Are you sure?" I asked, eyeing it skeptically. I turned to the kids. "Why don't you guys scoot your lawn chairs back a few feet just to be safe, okay?"

My brother poured the gasoline over the branches, and I knelt down and flicked my lighter. Suddenly, there was a loud explosion, and everything blew up in my face. Thick flames leapt into the air and onto my body as I staggered back in horror. Instantly, my mind went to the trauma training I'd received before working at the rehab center. I knew the kids were watching to see my reaction, and I had to play it cool.

"That was really weird, wasn't it?" I tried to laugh.

"Yeah, but your hair is on fire," one of the kids replied, pointing.

My mom jumped in and ushered the kids away from the scene. Suddenly, my entire body was overwhelmed with searing pain. I put my hand to my face, and when I pulled it back, my skin came right off with it. Terrified, I ran for the house and jumped in the shower, letting the cold water douse my burnt skin. The fire department showed up a few minutes later, followed by the paramedics, and they whisked me off in an ambulance.

I shook and screamed the entire 30-minute drive to the hospital. "Help me! Help me!" I cried, thrashing back and forth on the gurney.

The paramedic remained calm and helpful. He doused every towel he could find with cool water and applied them to my face and chest. "You're going to be okay," he assured me, giving me another shot of morphine. "We're almost there."

By the time we arrived at the hospital, I'd had nine shots of morphine. I spent the next three days in the hospital and the following month in bed. I'd received terrible second-degree burns to my face, chest, neck, arms and hands. Because my skin was now so thin, even the slightest scratch or touch would cause it to bleed. The doctors said it would take up to two months for me to fully recover. I thanked God that he had protected me, as I knew it could have been so much worse — fatal, even.

As I reeled from the experience, friends from church stepped up with meals, prayers and offers to help with

Dominic. I was so grateful for their kindness, and once again, I thanked God for giving me the courage to return to church. I couldn't imagine going through something this difficult without people like them to support me.

"I thought I was going to lose you, Hannah," Mario said when he came to visit one day. Concern was etched on his face, and I could see he was sincere. "Please, let's give us another chance. What do you say?"

"I'm willing, but I'm a different person now, Mario, and I want to see that you've changed, too," I told him.

After three months of trying to make things work, things were not going as I'd hoped.

"I think we need to break things off for good," I said. "I'm sorry."

"This is all your fault," Mario barked at me angrily. "I'm doing my part, being a good dad, trying to be good to you. What's your problem?"

I sighed. "Mario, I'll make a commitment to this relationship if you do, but I've asked you to change your behavior, and I'm not seeing the change I need. If you can't step up to the plate, I can't stick around."

Mario went silent and walked off. Deep down, I hoped things wouldn't work out. I was growing weary of our tumultuous relationship. We gave one last attempt to make the relationship work, but when he did not change his ways, I told him I was done for good.

In March 2011, I decided to take a trip to California to visit my brother. While I was away, Mario called every hour, demanding to know where I was. I had never seen such a controlling side of him before, and it frightened me.

"I told you we're done, Mario," I said, trying to remain calm. "Please leave me alone."

"I'll find you, Hannah," he threatened. "I'll hunt you down."

I hung up on him, my fingers shaking as I set down the phone.

Mario's behavior worsened by the summer. He constantly called and threatened me and even hacked into my accounts to gain personal information. Despite my constant pleas to leave me alone, he continued to harass me.

Meanwhile, I stayed involved on the worship team at my church. I loved being with my new friends and learning more about God through the Bible. I was finally in a good place and had discovered true joy, contentment and peace that only came through Jesus. I just wanted to move on with my life, but with Mario harassing me, I felt like someone was constantly stabbing me in the back and literally draining the life out of my body.

I hid Mario's abuse from my friends and family. My parents saw something in him they did not like and told me they wanted him out of my life for good. But I was in a bad spot financially and needed his help. I was also terrified that if I stood up to him, he would hurt me or even try to kill me. At last, exhausted from his irrational behavior, I confided in my best friend.

"Hannah, that's terrible! You need to get him to leave

you alone! You gotta set boundaries," she encouraged me.

"I know, you're right. Just pray for me to be strong. After all, he's Dominic's dad," I replied wearily.

One afternoon, he showed up at my house and frantically banged on the door. I finally threw open the door and stared him straight in the eye. "What are you doing here, Mario?" I demanded. "I told you not to come by and to leave me alone!"

"Who have you been calling, huh? I saw your phone records, and I know you've been calling other guys, haven't you?" His eyes were fiery as he glared at me.

"Mario, that is none of your business!" I screamed. "You leave me alone, or I'm calling the cops!"

"I know you're dating other guys," he went on angrily. "You're nothing but a prostitute, you know that? Those guys will never be a dad to your son!"

"I'm not looking for a dad for my son. I'm looking for peace of mind! Now do as I say, and leave me alone! For good! We are never, ever going to be together!" I slammed the door in his face.

Mario continued to harass me. Meanwhile, a cute guy named David started working at the church office. He was dating another girl, but we became friends, and I enjoyed his company.

On November 20, I went on a date with a new guy at a nearby Starbucks. Not long after I arrived, I glanced up from my coffee to see Mario storm in the door.

"What are you doing here with her?" Mario demanded to my date, getting in his face.

"Mario, what are *you* doing here?" I cried. "Get out and leave me alone! What I do with my personal time is none of your business!"

After a few more choice words, Mario stomped off, furious. I was shaken but tried to resume a conversation with my date. Later that evening, I went back to Mario's house to pick up Dominic. I took a deep breath as I walked to the door, knowing he was already angry with me.

To my horror, Mario marched toward me, threw me against the wall and dragged me into the bedroom.

"You're not so strong now, are you?" he sneered. He grabbed me and shoved me to the ground, then jabbed a gun into my neck.

I went completely limp and speechless, overcome by shock as I knelt there on the ground, the cold tip of the gun pressing into my skin as my veins pulsed in terror. I had seen the fury in his eyes, and I knew what he was thinking. He had every intention of killing me. In fact, he had already killed me in his mind.

Jesus. It was the only word that came to my mind. *Jesus, Jesus.* I repeated his name silently as I began to sob. *Jesus, please save me!*

"You're not going to keep me from my son, are you?" Mario asked, his breath hot against my face.

"No," I replied calmly, remembering my trauma training once again.

"You aren't going to date anyone else, are you?" he demanded next.

"No."

"And you aren't going to call the cops, are you?"

"No," I replied again. Inwardly, I was an utter wreck, but I kept my composure and hoped my steady voice did not portray my fear.

After nearly 45 minutes of torment, Mario finally put the gun down and slid it in his pocket. I stood up and raced to grab Dominic, who was screaming and crying nearby. I bolted for the front door, flew to my car, threw Dominic in the front seat and pressed down the lock just in time to see Mario charging toward me. Shaking uncontrollably, I shoved the car in reverse and peeled out of the parking lot as he ran after me.

My heart thudded in my chest as I sped away. Where could I go? I couldn't go home, as he knew where I lived. I thought quickly and then remembered I had friends who lived in a nearby apartment. I showed up at their house, banged on the door and collapsed on their couch when they let me in.

"Call the cops," I cried, breathlessly relaying the horrible story. The adrenaline drained from my body, and I felt like someone had just run me over with a semi-truck. When I heard sirens at last, I breathed a sigh of relief. I was going to be okay. Mario was not going to hurt me anymore.

The cops went to Mario's place after hearing my story and found six guns in his apartment. I tried to resume life, but it was difficult. Mario called everyone he knew and made up lies about the incident, turning the tables on me.

I tried to stay focused on God and reminded myself that he would pay for his actions. Justice was in God's hands now, not mine.

But it was difficult to play the piano again. Each time my fingers hit the keys, I froze up and the tears came.

God, why now? Why did this happen? I was doing so well and finally getting my confidence back. Where were you when all of this was happening? Is this just another consequence for what I did in the past? You have to answer me, God, you just have to!

But my cries were met with silence. I continued to cry out through my tears, begging God for answers. At last, I realized I might never know why it all had happened. I had to make a choice.

I could respond in anger and lash out at God with blame, or I could choose to trust in him and remember that he was still good.

God, I do trust you, I prayed. *I do still believe you are good. Please remind me of that when I feel alone and hopeless.*

As I continued to pour my heart out to God, I felt a sudden and very powerful presence in the room. I felt that Jesus was sitting right beside me as a protective husband would sit next to his wife. I started sobbing, thinking of the terrible experience I'd had at gunpoint. "Where were you?" I asked God.

And in that moment, I felt him say to me, *I was there, Hannah. I was between you and the gun. And my love for you is stronger than Mario's hatred.*

Stunned, I sat there, absorbing these words. I believe without a doubt they were from God. From that moment on, I let all fear slip away and chose to rely fully on God. To signify my newfound freedom, I got a tattoo with the words "There is no fear in love" on my shoulder. As a victim of trauma, I knew the first defense was to look for answers. But I had something better than answers — I had God on my side. The shackles that had held me down for so long were finally gone, replaced by a true joy that only came from within.

In February 2012, David invited me out on a motorcycle ride one day after work. As we sped around the beautiful Oregon countryside, the wind whipping our faces, we both suddenly realized we were having the time of our lives. We began dating, and within two weeks, I was certain he was the man God had chosen for me.

The next few months were filled with a newfound freedom and peace. I continued to struggle with my health, but when I visited a specialist, he performed some X-rays and discovered something surprising no other doctor had diagnosed until now.

I had hip dysplasia, a condition where joints are not formed correctly and the hip socket is too large and flat. Because of this, my hip was not properly held in place, causing the bone to bounce around and put stress on the muscles. This explained the pain I'd endured the past few years. I sought out a chiropractor, who recommended that I stand at a desk rather than sit to take the stress off my hip muscles.

I was grateful to have real answers at last so that I could move on. God was truly healing me emotionally, physically and spiritually.

᎒᎒᎒

On May 1 of that year, Mario went to trial for assault with a deadly weapon. He took a plea bargain and was sentenced to two and a half years in prison, followed by deportation back to Mexico. Relief flooded me as I realized Dominic and I would never have to see him again.

That summer, David and I took a camping trip to Astoria, Oregon, with his family. David had three girls from a previous relationship, and I adored them all. One warm afternoon, we climbed up a hundred steps to the top of a beautiful landmark column upon a hill. The Pacific Ocean lay below in full view, and we stood there for a moment, breathless, absorbing the beauty.

At the gift shop on the site, we all bought little wooden airplanes for a fundraiser to preserve the landmark. We each wrote something on our plane and then took turns throwing them off the hill. Just before David tossed his airplane into the air, he showed me what he'd written on it: "Will you marry me?"

I jumped up excitedly and threw my arms around him, responding with a loud "Yes!" that must have echoed for miles. Nothing had ever felt so right in my life.

On November 11, 2012, David and I were married at an old historic church in downtown Portland — 150 guests watched as I walked down the aisle. When I saw David standing at the altar, dashing in his crisp tuxedo, my heart did a tiny flip-flop. I had never felt so alive and beautiful as I stopped to face my soon-to-be husband before the crowd.

As we recited our vows, I was overwhelmed once again with a sense of true joy that came only from God. As a little girl, I had felt that joy when I played the piano and sang my heart out to the one who made me. But when ugly events took place, my heart shut down, leaving me with unspeakable pain. I felt defiled and worthless, but through God, I found hope and healing again. He put the song back in my heart and the music back in my soul. He restored me and reminded me over and over again that my past did not define me. In God's eyes, I was just the way David saw me now as I stood before him — a beloved one, cherished, beautiful, whole. I was free to sing again.

A SUNNY OUTLOOK
The Story of Sunshine Harmon
Written by Van S. Mabrito

The old man ambled by the crib. Pausing, he stood there with his stout white-skinned frame etched with tattoos. The Navy vet gazed down at the infant boy. *A brown baby … in MY family. That ain't right.* He started to walk away as he had every other time, but something made him pause.

The infant's eyes glistened like the sun's rays. He gurgled and cooed as the old man stood next to the crib. The boy's chubby arms reached with spastic moves as if seeking to touch — or be touched.

Suddenly, a tiny bronze hand wrapped around the old man's finger. The old vet bowed his head as he winced at the thought of his own prejudice, and a teardrop washed his cheek. He reached down and picked up the child, lifting him high above his head. As he eyed the lad, the boy smiled and cooed all the more. The old man smiled back. "Okay, Sunshine. Attaboy. You're a happy boy, aren't you?"

From that time on, Grandpa and I were fast buddies. We did everything together. Mom was single when she gave birth to me, so Grandpa quickly filled the void of the missing dad I never knew. Along with my mom, grandma, aunt and uncle, Grandpa became one of my main supporters. He was a great encourager and teacher during my early years. Ever since that time in my crib that I reached out to Grandpa for love and support, I've found myself continuing to reach out for those lifelines.

But I found out too late that some things I thought could strengthen me had the power to enslave and destroy me.

❧ ❧ ❧

Sunshine. Or Sunny. Yep, that's what my mom called me. That's my real name. But the name embarrassed me, and I preferred instead to be called by my middle name, Leon, until I got to college. Besides, I just didn't see myself as a Sunny, or a Leon, for that matter. I guess my name didn't seem right. Then again, maybe it was because I didn't have a dad around to tell me, "It's all right, son. You have a great name."

My mom did the best she could to raise me, but she had to work to support us. Mom was very nurturing and caring. She taught me right from wrong and valuable life lessons. I don't remember her ever raising her voice, but she knew how to share life's lessons with a tough love. One such incident took place when I was about 6 years old.

"Mom, I want to go to the park."

"No, son."

"That's not fair!" I stomped my foot.

"Son," she responded in her usual soft motherly tone, "life's not fair. Get that in your head."

Thankfully, my grandpa, grandma, aunt and uncle

were also around to help Mom carry the heavy load. In fact, we lived with my grandparents off and on during my early years in Seattle, and sometimes they stayed with us. I loved them both, as they loved me.

Grandma Esther modeled a textbook grandmother: We called her "the keeper of the flame," as she often shared great stories of our family history while she knitted and nurtured. She and I spent much time together. Grandpa James became the dad I never knew. He taught me how to use tools and play golf. He took me to practice when I played sports and to the hospital when I broke my nose playing baseball. He even took me once or twice a week to the Mariners' baseball games.

"Hey, Sunny, want some more popcorn?" Grandpa handed me the bag as the Navy anchor tattoo on his arm protruded out of his sleeve. The Mariners were up to bat.

"Thanks, Grandpa."

"Third base is coming up. Do you think he's going to bunt?"

"Yeah, I think he will." Grandpa knew baseball, but I felt good that he asked me my opinion.

Although Grandpa never seemed particularly religious, he represented the closest example I knew of a man of faith. He didn't cuss or drink, and he was as honest as they come. The proverbial strong, silent type, my granddad portrayed a good salt-of-the-earth man. He had a good head on his shoulders. After his stint in the Navy followed by piloting a tugboat, he worked as an accountant for the American Can Company before retiring. Retirement didn't stop Grandpa. He went and started his own coin shop.

Uncle Hans and Aunt Phyllis rounded out my extended support family. Since they only lived two blocks away, Mom and I visited them often — but each visit was special. I frequently traveled with them to Whidbey Island in the Puget Sound where we walked the beach together.

My grandparents were never absent from my life. Mom was, of course, there as well — except when she had to work. She worked on an assembly line at the Boeing plant for years. That is, until Boeing's big layoff in 1971. She did whatever work she could to make ends meet for us. She even delivered phonebooks for a while.

Seattle was a great place to grow up. A kid could play with his friends until dark back then and return home safe. Above all, I had a close-knit and loving extended family — so much so that I didn't always seem to notice that I didn't have a dad.

We moved from Seattle to Everett when Mom and her then-boyfriend bought a Mini Mart there. Then, the rude hand of death struck my family and me. Grandma died suddenly and unexpectedly. Grandpa was lost without her. The loss hit me hard as well. One of my main supports was gone. Even worse, when Grandpa remarried, he moved out of our house into a condo farther away, and I didn't see him as often.

࿇࿇࿇

"Harmon, get over here!" The booming loud voice echoed off of the wooden floor and throughout the gym.

I ran off the court and up to Coach Jefferies. "Yes, sir?"

"Harmon — you *have* to get after the ball. You *can't* make mistakes like that!" His sharp, impatient tone cut like a knife. Sure, I had missed a pass, and the basketball had flown through my hands. *But it's just a game. It's just sports. It's not the end of the world!*

People like Coach Jefferies mistook my laidback, easygoing personality for laziness — as if I didn't care. But I did. When I found something I liked, I threw myself into it with passion and dedication. I loved sports in high school: football, basketball and track. Win or lose, after a game, I was okay with whatever happened — as long as I knew I did my best. Regardless of how hard I tried, it sometimes didn't seem to be enough for the coaches.

I stood off court and watched my teammates scrimmage. Jimmy stood like a statue as the ball flew between his hands.

"Wilson," Coach Jeffries spoke reassuringly, "that's okay. Just get after that."

The difference in the way the coaches treated me compared to the other kids stung. Everett High School only had three or four brown kids. My head fell in discouragement, and my brown arms and hands stuck out before me. I felt like salt was being rubbed into my wounds. *It's just a game, coach! Just a game ... or is there something wrong with me? Do I need to do something to make me more of a go-getter?* I wondered. And I wondered again, *Maybe it's not the color of my skin. Can they tell what I'm doing? Do they know my secret?*

Yet, despite my weaknesses — and the secret I held inside — I managed to be elected as president of the high school's Boy's Club, a leadership and service organization. Those responsibilities and my involvement in sports boosted my confidence and lent structure to my life. Like an unseen hand, my passion kept me in line — at least for a while. I've often heard that the friends we keep greatly determine our direction in life. Looking back over my life, I've found that some friends truly don't deserve that kind of power over our lives.

☙☙☙

I poked at the fire with a stick, and a plume of ash and smoke rose into the chilly morning air.

"Leon, put another log on the fire," Bill charged me as he fanned the flames with his hand and blew on them.

I compliantly went to the wood stack and grabbed a log. Then I carefully set it on top of the pyre. Flames and smoke rose higher, puncturing some of the cold as Bill, his friend Ted and I sat huddled around the warmth.

Bill was a year older than me. He was the son of my mom's boyfriend, Dan, and Mom and I had moved in with Dan and Bill. I had just begun high school, and we had met them here in little Gold Bar, Washington, to camp in Dan's three-wheel trailer. Mom and Dan had left earlier in the morning to play cards or something with

A SUNNY OUTLOOK

other campers in the trailer campgrounds. Mom didn't always make the best choices in boyfriends. Now the other boys and I were alone.

I looked up and saw Bill and Ted passing a marijuana joint back and forth as each took a puff and exhaled. Acting oblivious to me, they continued their ritual. Finally, Bill looked up at me with the smoldering joint between his thumb and finger.

"You want to try it now?" He nonchalantly held it out to me.

Whenever Bill asked me before, I had said no. He never really pressured me. He just offered, and I had declined. I had no real friends then. I always felt like the oddball. So as we sat together around the warmth of the campfire, I found myself reaching out to accept his offer. "Okay."

My family would never have allowed me to use drugs. But I didn't have a dad to tell me "Good job, son" the first few times I refused drugs. Or to say "Don't do it" with love but firmness when temptation tried to barge in. Nor did I have the right kind of friends to turn me away from drugs. I couldn't talk to my mom. She wouldn't understand — and she had her own problems.

But my using didn't stop then. That brisk morning began my first slide down into doing drugs and drinking recreationally that continued through my high school years. Drugs gave me the strength and confidence I needed to do what I needed to do — including sports — without being held back by my easygoing personality. Or so I thought. A strong man may actually be a hollow man under an illusion. Soon my heart was pumping on near empty, except for this secret I now carried. I continued to reach out for a helping hand.

సఞసఞసఞ

"Sunshine Leon Harmon." As the principal recited my name in ceremonial cadence, I proudly stepped out and marched across the auditorium stage, shook his hand and received my diploma. In May of 1986, I had successfully completed high school. But I wanted to keep on marching.

One month later, I packed up my belongings and headed for Phoenix, Arizona. I just had to go. I had big dreams, and I didn't think they would blossom in little Everett, Washington. Mom also had big dreams for me, but she didn't think Phoenix would bring about the best for her son. Even though that's what she thought, she didn't say much.

"You know, it's not too late to change your mind ..."

"I know."

"Drive carefully, and don't forget to write."

"I will, I promise."

We hugged and kissed each other goodbye. Then I hopped into my brown '77 Chevy Camaro Z28. As I backed out of the driveway and waved goodbye, I saw under her smile a concerned look.

DeVry University in Phoenix had recruited on my high school campus, and I was accepted into the school's computer programming degree plan. Even though I wanted to make something of my life, that degree seemed the easiest. But completing a four-year degree in about two and a half years turned out to be more intensive than I reckoned, and now I had no family support nearby.

Later the next year, my friend and fellow student John and I chowed down in the university cafeteria. He came from Alaska, and the two of us hit it off as soon as we met. The drab, sterile university dining hall that seemed more like a hospital cafeteria contrasted with John's bright enthusiasm.

"Hey, Sunny!" John spoke with excitement. "I got invited to a church last week. It was pretty cool. Why don't you come with me Sunday?"

The next Sunday, John and I marched into a little church on the rough side of Phoenix. I looked around. The quaint building appeared to be out of a movie: earth-tone walls surrounding long, hard wooden pews resting on an old-fashioned wood floor. The people seemed very friendly as they greeted us. We sat near the front but just observed. I enjoyed the music and the pastor's talk.

The next week I returned. At the end of the pastor's preaching, he called out to the congregation.

"If anyone here wants to be forgiven for the things you've done wrong and commit your life to the Lord, then come down here. Let me pray with you."

I wasn't using drugs and alcohol at this time. And I did believe in God in a way. But for some reason, now I became aware of God's reality. And I wanted to do what he wanted me to do. So among about 300 people, I went forward to let the pastor pray with me.

He warmly greeted me and asked me my name. As he placed his hands on my shoulders, he encouraged me to just talk to God from my heart. He asked me to pray and repeat his words, asking God to forgive me for the things I had done wrong. I did so, and suddenly the people started clapping. Then many of them stepped forward and greeted me with happy, enthusiastic high-fives and hugging.

I started attending the church three to four times a week. Participation in the church, the people I met, the things I heard there, it all made my life feel more exciting somehow. Then a family headed up by a single mom with three daughters and a son invited me to stay in their home. Betty, the mom, reached out to help me since I had neither a job nor an apartment at the time. This provision of a place to stay seemed to be a real godsend. Betty and her kids made me feel at home. And they were very religious — *very*.

Soon I began doing everything I felt I was supposed to do: I was baptized, continued attending church regularly, prayed and read my Bible. I even fasted, giving up food in order to draw close to God. My life seemed to be going smoothly. Eventually, I found work and was able to pay Betty some rent. Then she launched me out of the security of her home.

"Sunny, now you've got enough income. It's time to go do your own thing."

So I found a place of my own, but the apartment put me on the other side of town, far from Betty and the church, which made it easier to start skipping services. With my family far away and my church support network weakening with my increased absences, it became harder to feel connected. Despite my religious enthusiasm, I never had developed a real relationship with God. My spiritual life had become reduced to a laundry-list of do's and don'ts. I didn't have a true spiritual foundation. I just plain struggled to do life.

Okay, what will I have for breakfast? Popcorn, cereal or potatoes? I had cereal and popcorn the last time ... guess I'll go for the potatoes now.

My number one mission was just to survive in the world. So my life drifted further and further from God — and stability. I got to a point where I was treading the waters of baptism and felt I was going under.

ॐॐॐ

Something cold and metallic was suddenly poking into the back of my head. Man, was I upset! A thought flashed through my mind: *Can't they see I'm trying to get some work done?!* And just as I turned to give the prankster a piece of my mind, I heard the gruff voice roar, "Get off the phone!"

Suddenly, I realized I was in the middle of a robbery. The gunman directed me to an adjacent room where three fellow employees already lay facedown on the ground.

Then he barked at me, "Lay down on the ground ... facedown! Now!"

I got down as quickly as I could, as the main thug's accomplice nervously but triumphantly squealed, "Let's smoke 'em!"

The moments of silence that followed seemed to last an eternity.

I worked as a bellman for the Holiday Inn at the Phoenix Sky Harbor Airport, while studying at the community college before I entered Northern Arizona. I had just sat down to do some paperwork in a backroom when I took the phone call — and was so rudely interrupted.

With my face riveted to the carpet, my ears keenly picked up the sounds of footsteps mingled with flesh being patted down. *When will this be over?* I heard one robber wrestling with something on the counter behind me. Suddenly I momentarily felt the heat of legs straddling over me and rank breath falling on my neck. Then I felt my wallet quickly slipping out of my back pocket like it was greased.

As suddenly as the robbery had begun, the room loomed over us still and quiet. I ventured to take a peek and saw that the thieves had vanished. We all arose and dusted ourselves off, thankful they hadn't taken our lives — only our wallets. And the whole cash register, I noticed. I wondered something else as well.

Is God trying to get my attention?

A SUNNY OUTLOOK

స్తిస్తిస్తి

It had been a couple of years since I'd regularly attended church. I'd continued to work while I studied at Mesa Community College, where I ran track competing in the decathlon. I had some level of success, but working multiple jobs and full-time school just didn't permit the proper dedication. I remember some terms being on the Dean's List and some on academic probation. As in my youth, sports now kept me out of trouble and provided me with a coach to guide me somewhat. I had always dreamed of being a Washington Husky. Now, I reached for that dream.

Seattle was Husky turf, and I grew up only two miles from the University of Washington campus. I lived and dreamed of attending that school. So I applied for entrance to the U of W and waited ... and waited.

Nothing. I heard nothing from them. I was crestfallen. *I didn't make it. Guess I wasn't good enough.*

So I resigned myself to applying for admission to Northern Arizona University in Flagstaff. Then I received the notice: I was accepted to NAU! Relief. Gladness. Until another notice allayed my happiness.

That morning I envisioned myself walking past the 100-year-old red sandstone Romanesque building called Old Main. Today I was scheduled to enroll for the fall 1990 semester at the NAU main campus nestled among Ponderosa pines. Skimming through my mail before I left my apartment, I was jerked to attention by one return address. The official-looking envelope read "The University of Washington." Breathless, I quickly tore open the envelope.

"We are happy to inform you that you have been accepted for the autumn quarter 1990 of the University of Washington."

I fell, stunned, into a nearby chair. *Accepted to two universities. One, my dream school. What am I going to do?*

I did what I'd planned that morning and found myself piercing the forest of Ponderosas and marching past stately Old Main to enroll at Northern Arizona University. I focused on my studies and worked hard, preparing for graduation. Things felt uncomplicated, good. That is, until one fall day in 1992.

The day already had me down — and almost out. My landlord had served me eviction papers, and I had lost my two roommates. The plain white walls and tan carpet of my apartment stuck out amidst the sparse remnants of furniture left.

Brrring. Having no chair to sit on, I stood up as I answered the phone.

"Hello?"

"Sunny!" the familiar voice said. "This is Aunt Phyllis."

I could tell by the urgency in her voice something was wrong. In fact, it had been some time since I had spoken to anyone in the family, being so caught up in the life of a student. I knew I should have been writing or calling once in a while. I hadn't even given Grandpa a ring lately.

A SUNNY OUTLOOK

"Sunny," my aunt pressed on. "I have some bad news."
I braced myself.

"Grandpa died yesterday."

"What-t-t-t!" My voice grew weak. I paced the floor, and my eyes darted back and forth between the bare walls and the window view, trying to comprehend the words I heard.

"He had a heart attack and crashed his car." Her voice trembled. Of course she was distressed — Grandpa was her stepdad. "He probably died before the car crashed."

Her words hit me like a stun gun.

"There's going to be a memorial service."

"Aunt Phyllis, I can't. I've got classes, and I don't have the money to come home."

"Don't worry about it — you do what you have to do. Keep in touch."

After Aunt Phyllis and I hung up, I stood all alone. Tears flowed down my cheeks as I stared out the window into nothingness. *Grandpa. My grandpa.* My breath hung still, as if a knife had pierced my lungs. Memories flashed before my mind. Times Grandpa had placed his big, strong hands on mine and guided me in sawing a piece of wood with a handsaw. Or when I stood on the greens with his solid tattooed frame enveloping me to show me how to hold a putter and put his magic touch on the ball. Grandpa offering me popcorn at the Mariners' games.

"Do you think he'll bunt?"

Now I was alone — except for a flash flood of a thousand thoughts and emotions. Sure, my granddad was the silent type and rarely reached out. *But why didn't I call him more often? I never got to have a real man-to-man talk with him. I'd like to have known him better — there are so many things I didn't know about him.* Feelings of sorrow and grief were soon accompanied by hordes of other emotions: guilt, regret, remorse, self-doubt ... and self-accusations.

I can't even make the funeral.

Somehow, I managed to graduate from Northern Arizona University in December of 1993. The occasion that should have been a springboard of hope only became a blind leap off the diving board into darker and more turbulent waters than I had ever known.

窰窰窰

After graduation, a series of mishaps and missteps should have awakened me to the reality that I wasn't steering my life very wisely. I never seemed to listen to the voice trying to tell me, *Hey, Sunny. I'd like to take over the steering wheel.* Not after the holdup at the hotel. Not when my grandpa died. No, I kept on. I never knew when I took a step if I would fall into a dark hole immediately in front of me. On the other hand, the biggest hole seemed to be in my heart.

"Hey, man. Can you give us a ride?" Two beefy guys came up to me at a bar in Flagstaff. I had just ordered another one-too-many and slammed my combo money clip-knife on the bar counter. I tried to size up the two through my fuzzy thoughts. Most locals knew each other in our area, but I didn't recognize these guys. They seemed friendly enough — as best as I could tell.

"Sure, no problem," I slurred. I chugged my brew, turned from the bar and steadied myself as I walked toward the exit door. The two men followed.

We piled into my 1980s brown square-bodied Volvo with four doors and crank window handles. This car meant *FREEDOM*: freedom to get to work and get around. And I had gotten my Volvo for only $500.

One man sat in the seat beside me, the other remained hidden in the darkness of the backseat. I plopped my money clip-knife on the dashboard, and we headed out. Other than Route 66 in Flagstaff, I didn't pay much attention to the streets they directed me through. Suddenly, I found myself on a dark side street in a strange, quiet neighborhood. An alarm went off in my head.

"Say, man. Where are we?" I turned my head to see the guy on my right holding my knife up to my face.

"Here's the deal — we want your car. Get out now," he commanded.

I opened the door and stepped out as the two mirrored my movements, and the lead guy continued to hold the knife up to me. Suddenly rage filtered through my foggy mind.

No way — I just put new speakers in!

"You lousy b*****ds. You lousy pieces of s***. You're not getting my car." I suddenly reached down into my car and grabbed the keys with my right hand.

Then I saw the flash of steel. I instinctively thrust up my left hand to protect myself as my own knife slashed my fingers and blood spewed out. The two robbers turned and hightailed it. I laughed on the inside. *You b*****ds didn't get my car.*

I felt quite proud of myself for saving my Volvo — until I got the tab for the emergency room surgery to stitch up the severed tendons and nerves on three fingers: $1,500 — *per finger.* Ouch! That hurt.

To make matters worse, with my hand injury, I couldn't even work. I floundered without direction or goals, idle. Again, I was at a fork in the road. If I had realized it, I would have heard the little voice still trying to tell me, *Hey, Sunny? Can't you see your way is not working?*

So for those 12 years after I graduated from NAU, my life was total "FTT": Failure To Thrive. I continued to drink and smoke pot, and I quickly graduated to acid and meth. Soon, I was addicted.

A former Vietnam vet, now turned dealer, told me about his being hooked on heroin and meth.

"No, man. Meth is way worse. I got off heroin a lot easier."

I thought about it — but only for a moment. Drugs gave me the confidence I lacked, the strength to do what I had to do. I didn't realize that some dark force had tested me with one drug after another to find the one that tapped into my insecurity about my easygoing, laidback nature. *Man, I want to be a go-getter. This stuff does the trick —*

helps me do what I need to do. After a friend got me turned onto meth, finding others that were doing the same thing wasn't hard.

The path of destruction of my relationships, time and money progressed with painful devastation, including DUIs and 15 days in jail for fighting and drinking. At one point, I thought I found a light and reached out again. Even little lights, however, have their limits.

☙ ☙ ☙

I stepped behind the bar of the tavern I managed in Northwest Portland and reached down to stow a dirty glass. As I stood up, I saw her sitting at the bar. Her eyes met mine.

Wow! I thought to myself. My mouth dropped. As we talked, I tried to think of a way to take her out to eat and drink.

Lana and I soon started dating. About a year and a half after Lana and I met, Bo entered our lives. Then I moved into her house with her daughter, Aidan, who was still in a stroller.

The birth of Bo was fantastic. His entrance excited me — the best feeling ever. But the responsibilities stressed me greatly, and they scared me. I never had siblings — and now I didn't know how to be a dad. Though I loved Bo, I didn't know how I could afford to support a child. Once again, I needed more confidence. I would have been more confident about getting into an airplane and piloting it for the first time coast-to-coast. At least I would know if I got it right or wrong. I found that when you're raising a child, you don't always get feedback on whether you've made the right — or wrong — choices.

On top of that, I began the purchase of a pressure washing business. Cleaning houses and dump trucks seemed simple enough. But the demands and long hours put the pressure on me. That nagging dark voice again convinced me that I needed the meth to keep going and get the job done. At first, I used at work and for work. At its peak, my addiction clamored for me from dawn until dusk. When I tried quitting, the three or four days of withdrawal hit me hard — and left me without energy to do the most basic tasks. I would just eat and sleep. And I would hear the whisper: *See, you can't quit. You can't do without it. You are going to die just like this.*

So I continued to try to fill my heart hole with drugs. But Lana's and my relationship seemed to be going well, in spite of my using. Or so I thought.

"Get out of here. I want you out of my house — NOW!" Lana screamed at me.

"But, Lana …"

"No, I've had enough of your lying. Get out!"

"Please give me another chance."

"No, I've given you plenty of chances. I don't trust you anymore."

I knew she was right. By this time, I lived in her basement because my lying and excuses had shattered Lana's trust in me. I'd been lying to myself. I couldn't give

100 percent to Lana when I also double-timed with a girl named Meth.

Now my true love had had enough of the lying — about drugs, about pornography … about everything. I was completely out now.

I moved out and found my own house and a roommate. I continued to work my business while the meth worked me. I still couldn't stop, and my days wore dark like the night.

Thankfully, Lana still allowed me to see Bo two or three times a week, but only because she believed I wasn't using. I would drive over to her house to watch him while she went to work. This little light flickered in the wind and darkness of this stormy season — until I overslept.

I had been working long, hard hours in my business — sometimes as late as 4 a.m. — with the help of my juice to keep my system revved up. My system couldn't take it anymore, and neither could Lana. When I didn't show up that morning, Lana had had enough. She put her foot down. I wouldn't see Bo anymore. My nightlight went out — as did my hope. I didn't realize it then, but despite all the failures and foolishness, a great light — a light brighter than the sun — was about to shine in Sunshine Harmon's life.

෴෴෴

"Sunny, here's the deal." Lana's voice was stern and firm on the phone.

I paused timidly to hear what she had to say.

"I know you want to see Bo, but I can't trust you. You can see Bo ..." She paused long enough to get my attention. I missed her, but I was desperate to see Bo. My ears and my heart were wide open.

"I've decided you can see Bo, but only on scheduled days — and under supervision."

On my appointed day, I nervously walked into the drab Child Protective Services office. I looked around at the strangers and unfamiliar faces. *This is ridiculous!* A huge wave of emotions hit me. Anger. Outrage. Helplessness. Feeling victimized. Then guilt. Big guilt. *My addictions. It's my addictions ... and my fault.* I knew it was true.

But Lana and I somehow managed to start reconciling. On a July night in 2005, I drove over to her house for dinner. Lana asked me to take Bo swimming after we ate. She took him upstairs to brush his teeth and came back down. I had disappeared. She went outside to look for me and discovered me sitting in my truck — smoking meth.

"Get out of here! And don't come back!" Lana shouted at me.

As I drove home, I felt horrible — and guilty. *What have I done? How did I get here?* My mind turned my life choices and events over and over, like a huge computer processing vast amounts of data. The evidence against me was devastating.

The next morning I walked back and forth from the garage to the Ford truck putting my tools in for work. *I've got to get my life right!* But I knew I couldn't do it on my own. Several years before, I had an encounter with Jesus Christ at the church I had visited in South Phoenix. I knew that God sent Jesus to earth to live and die. I knew he did it so that all of us could be forgiven for the things we've done wrong and receive eternal life. I had prayed then to ask Jesus into my life, but my supposed Christian life mainly consisted of trying to keep up with a list of all the things I was supposed to do. I, however, never truly knew Jesus in a personal relationship. This time I didn't pray formally — or as a ritual. I cried out for help. I stopped walking and started talking — to a God and Jesus I had long forgotten. I spoke to him as if he was right there — and he was.

"Lord, I know you're there." The dark shadows of my wasted life stood before me like a black-robed judge before a condemned man. But I pressed on. "I believe in you." I paused and thought back over my life. When I was young, I'd always had a sense that I would do something great with my life. "I know this isn't what you planned for me. And I know I really screwed up. I want to change. I want to quit. But I can't do it by myself. Show me what to do!" I was desperate.

My heart and my mind were resolved: I would rather be crushed trying to quit or end up panhandling than be crushed as an addict. I knew I needed the power of God to make it. Suddenly, I felt a bit more confident than I'd felt in a long time. *Well, we'll just see what happens.*

The first two days hit me hard and horribly. Now,

however, I knew that the whispering creature of the dark only lied whenever he'd jerked my chain and sneered, *You can't make it without drugs.* I began going to work clean. My confidence gradually came back — a confidence I hadn't known since being a kid with Grandpa and the family. The challenge was difficult, but not impossible with the Lord's help. I found myself able to do things I thought I couldn't do without drugs and do them better! *I can work my business without the meth.* I had made up my mind to get free, but I knew above all that the power of Christ had transformed and liberated me. Jesus had shone his light on the whispering one, the devil — and my eyes saw the devil for who he is: a big liar who long ago rebelled against God's love and now only sought to kill and destroy those who Jesus came to rescue.

Now I was confident and free. Free to live life to the fullest — and to love.

ॐॐॐ

I knew Jesus had made me a new man. But old scars don't heal easily. I knew my reckless living had devastated Lana's trust in me, but she and I began the journey of healing and reconciliation.

Every family is a work in progress, and ours was no exception. Neither was my life. Even a changed man needs time to grow and be fully transformed. Oh, and I still had my rough edges. Whenever I became worked up about work, my new grounding in God would remind me that

A SUNNY OUTLOOK

my business is not my first job. The Lord taught me the important priorities of life: God, family and then work — in that order.

A miracle happened with the love of my life on a bright Valentine's Day in 2010. As Lana and I held each other's hands and gazed into each other's eyes, we heard the ancient benediction announced over us: "I now pronounce you husband and wife. You may kiss the bride."

That special day took place at Anthem, a church where I'm often reminded that anyone's story can be transformed, as mine was. It's a place (and a community of loving people) that God continues to use in my life and marriage. All my life I'd hungered for someone to be there — to give support and encouragement. And right away Pastor Brad, his wife, Lisa, and the people of Anthem took us in as family. The marriage and parenting small groups have helped our family tremendously. And through the men's retreats, I've built deep companionship in this new life with other men, who've become like brothers to me in Christ, and have seen how they, too, experienced the Lord leading them through trials to triumph.

"What was your relationship with your dad like?" I asked my friend Calvin, a successful family man and professional, at a men's retreat as I cast my fishing line into the lake. I expected Cal to recount the nurturing, mentoring role that his father played and that they still share a close and meaningful bond to this day.

Cal tugged at his line and then let it settle in the water.

"I don't really know him," he shared. "He used to beat up on my mom pretty bad, then he got to me pretty good one time — and my mom got me out of there."

Wow. Cal had a father scar on his heart. I had a father hole. I was thankful my wound was not more severe. And I'm even more thankful that God is not just my Lord but my dad, who can restore all things — for anyone.

I am especially thankful for my family. I get to talk with Bo about God and get a glimpse through his 10-year-old eyes, and then I get to discuss the more advanced, difficult dynamics of the Christian experience with Lana. Aidan, my 15-year-old stepdaughter, also is a joy to be around. She comes to work with me occasionally, and we always talk about God. I delight in our discussions because we compare ideas that we gain from church and from living in today's world.

"Ya' know, Sunny, this world must be so confusing for people without God in their lives." Aidan's voice was tinged with a note of sadness.

"Yep," I reflected, "I think you're right." I always feel so lucky, and I have to remind myself that it's not luck, but that my life is a gift from our generous God.

All my family members are quite observant, and they bring so very much that I would never think of on my own. They are as much a part of my "Sunny-ness" as I am myself. They mean everything to me.

I do have another love in my life. It's nowhere near my love for my heavenly dad, my family or even my work. The first time I sported my gi and began sparring, I loved martial arts. I tried practicing the discipline before I began my journey with Jesus, and like everything else in my life at that time, I thought I needed drugs to help me do it. But when Jesus came into my life and drugs went out, I found I did better in martial arts as well: I began to win tournaments. I even earned my black belt in Kajukenbo, the original mixed martial art. More importantly, the Lord used martial arts to build even greater confidence — and to teach me important life lessons.

Life is a battle at times. Sometimes the giants we face can appear impossible to defeat — as Goliath towered over a young David who would eventually become king of Israel, according to the Bible. Teenage David stood before the battle-hardened giant who had slain warriors far bigger, stronger and more experienced than a little shepherd boy from the hills of Judea. Likewise, my Goliath of insecurity, an absent father and powerful drug addictions seemed impossible to conquer. The giant in my life appeared certain to slay me. Even a professional counselor had told me that I couldn't just quit my addictions — that I needed an inpatient program to help. "Statistically, it is virtually unheard of for someone to use meth for more than a decade and successfully quit using this drug," the counselor told me matter-of-factly. My lack of both insurance and finances made professional intervention impossible. But like David, I learned that nothing is impossible with God and his power.

☙❧☙

Ten-year-old Bo and I were horse-playing on the floor of our living room. Suddenly, the voice of the newscaster on our TV caught my attention.

"Two people shot to death at a mall in suburban Portland; the masked gunman also dies. That story coming up next."

I turned to Bo and leaned down to him. I always want to make sure that I'm the best dad I can be for him and that he knows I'm always there for him. To be sure that he has the support of his father. I give him the best advice I can to prepare him for life, even though I know I'm not perfect.

"Son, pay attention. Sometimes things will happen in life that you didn't plan for. You have to be prepared. You have to be on your feet." Bo looked up at me with his trusting eyes. "You have to be prepared both spiritually *and* physically. Do you understand, Bo?" He nodded his head. I continued. "I can teach you martial arts, and that is good. You can defend yourself with that. But sometimes things come at you that are so big that you need Papa God's power and protection. Do you understand, son?"

Bo's face appeared puzzled.

"Son, if I lie to someone ... if I don't keep my promise to him or if I do something to harm him, then I've not only hurt him, but I've hurt God — and myself as well. Anything we do that hurts someone makes God sad and is called sin."

Bo listened intently. I continued. "And sin hurts, destroys and kills — just like a man with a gun who shoots someone. I can defeat it one of two ways." I slapped my chest and instructed Bo, "Throw me a punch."

He cocked his little right arm and tried to wallop my chest.

I held up my open hand and caught his punch. "See, you can block it. Or … throw me another punch."

Bo hauled off and threw another punch at my chest. This time, I leaned back and away as his punch flew by me.

"Or, son, you can get away from those things that hurt other people and yourself — and stay free." I looked into his face. "Does that make sense, Bo?"

"Yes, Dad."

I smiled at him, and he smiled back big. And we hugged each other.

"I love you very much, son."

"I love you, Dad."

Suddenly, a memory flashed across my mind. Grandpa's big frame covered me as I held the golf club back, ready to swing. Then his strong arms became one with mine as I drove the ball farther down the green than I ever had.

"Attaboy, Sunny! See — you can do it!"

"Wow!" I turned to Grandpa. "I did it, Grandpa!"

He smiled at me. "You sure did, Sunny."

"Dad?" Bo's voice awoke me from my daydream.

"Yes, son?"

"I'm hungry."

"How about a sandwich?"

"Yeah!" Bo replied enthusiastically. His hand reached out and took mine.

We turned and headed to the kitchen. As we did, the newscast caught my ear again.

"Okay, folks, now for your weekend forecast. Good news!" The weatherman spoke with a chipper tone. "You're going to have calm winds, clear skies and the outlook is sunny."

A RAINBOW OF PROMISE
The Story of Janelle Ireland
Written by Karen Koczwara

"Josh is dead! You need to get over here now!" I screamed when my mother answered the phone, my words tumbling out in a rush.

The phone rang. This time, it was my husband returning my call. "Josh isn't breathing! You need to come home!" I yelled frantically. I collapsed on the gravel driveway, screaming and crying as the paramedics worked on my tiny son a few feet away.

How could this be happening? Surely, this was all just a bad dream. I had left little Joshua sleeping peacefully in the bed, and now he was lying in the back of an ambulance! Time stood still as I waited for my husband to arrive. My mind was raging.

Please let this all be a mistake! Please don't let him be gone!

There had already been so much loss — the other babies, who I never got to hold. The doctors had said I might never conceive again. Joshua was our miracle baby. And now we needed just that — a miracle — to save this little boy.

❧ ❧ ❧

Some folks describe Portland, Oregon, as a bustling big city with small-town charm. Nestled in the Northwest where the Columbia and the Willamette Rivers meet, Portland's landscape is as eclectic as those who call it home. Museums, coffee shops and both upscale and hole-in-the-wall eateries line the downtown streets, and lush greenery pokes through the urban concrete. College students bundle in scarves and mingle on the corners, while businessmen in suits brush elbows with vagrants as they pass them by. For some, Portland is an escape, a place to blend in with the crowd and disappear. For others, it's a place where dreams and burdens collide. But for me, it is simply the place I've called home for 27 years.

I was born on April 22, 1985; my brother, Ryan, was two years older. My father was a brilliant man who held a bachelor's in biochemistry; he moved to Oregon from Northern California for school. After my parents married, my father went to work for a large department store, while my mother held down a job as an office receptionist. Our first home was a modest two-bedroom place in a four-plex; my grandparents lived next door. With hardwood floors, a full basement and a makeshift laundry chute, the little house provided plenty of adventure for my older brother and me.

I was a precocious child, always curious, delving into mischief and getting the paddle on my bottom when I misbehaved. I often tried my mother's patience when I begged for treats at the grocery store, and after I stole a pack of gum, she refused to take me with her anymore. I put my entrepreneurial skills to use when I got a bit older, crafting bookmarks out of paper and yarn and selling them door-to-door. Barbie dolls were high on my wish list, but my parents weren't big fans, so I spent most of my time playing outside with my brother making up our own games.

In many ways, we were the average American family. Though my parents worked long hours, my grandparents cared for us when they were away; we became very close. At night, I always looked forward to my mother's steaming hot homemade pizzas for dinner. And when I drifted off to sleep, my father sat at the foot of my bed and sang "Thank Heaven for Little Girls" and "Swing Low, Sweet Chariot" in his low, soothing voice.

We attended church each Sunday, and I liked it well enough. When I entered kindergarten, my parents enrolled me in Portland Christian School. I loved my new friends, my teacher and the classes. I know it was a stretch for my parents to keep me there financially, but they were determined to provide a wholesome, healthy environment for me.

We moved to a two-story three-bedroom home in the Northeast suburbs of Portland in 1991. Though the place was much bigger than our first home, it needed considerable work, and my parents spent years remodeling it. Just before I entered junior high, we took in a girl named Shannon. She and I soon became best friends and called ourselves sisters. We shared a room upstairs next to my parents so they could keep a close eye on us.

In seventh grade, I began to gravitate toward the wrong crowd. I grew bored with my Christian school and faked a fight with a girl on campus so I could get kicked out. My parents put me in public school, where Shannon and I made even more trouble. We harassed the teachers and played mean tricks on them, sticking condoms on their backs when they weren't looking. I refused to do my schoolwork, and my parents and teachers all grew increasingly frustrated with me.

"Psst. Wanna ditch class with me after lunch?" my friend asked me one morning.

"Sure. Meet you in the hall," I whispered back.

Instead of heading to math class that afternoon, we slipped out of the building and wandered down the street toward the local bowling alley. When we arrived in the parking lot, my friend pulled out a joint and offered it to me. "You ever smoke weed?" she asked.

I shrugged. "I do now," I replied coolly. The smoke burned my lungs as I inhaled, but I liked the pleasant buzz that followed moments later. "You got more of that?" I asked.

"There's always more," she said, laughing.

When the coast was clear, my friend showed me how to break into the cars in the parking lot by jimmying the locks. "Never know what kind of loot you'll find," she said. "Kinda like Christmas, ya know?"

There was something slightly thrilling about the idea of breaking all the rules. I'd always been an impish child, curious about the world outside my Christian church and school. Though the days of my spankings and my father's stern reminders about right and wrong were firmly planted in my memory, the adrenaline rush that followed an act of rebellion was somewhat delicious and even harder to forget.

When I was 14, I discovered online chatting. With just a few clicks, I could correspond with cute guys all over the country. Shannon and I struck up several conversations and enjoyed flirting back and forth with our new boyfriends.

Soon, I worked up the courage to call a guy I'd met online who lived in Canada, and we talked for hours in the privacy of my room.

One day, I came home to find my mother holding a paper, a horrified look on her face. "Janelle, do you have an explanation for why we just got a $1,000 phone bill in the mail?" she asked, her eyes fiery as they bore into mine.

I gulped hard. "Um, sorry … I might have, uh, made a few phone calls to a guy out of state," I mumbled.

She shook her head. "Well, I certainly hope we can get this straightened out. Don't do that ever again, young lady."

But a few weeks later, another phone bill came — this one for a whopping $7,000! I had neglected to research the steep 77-cent-a-minute long-distance fees before calling Canada. My parents were furious, and I vowed never to do something so foolish again.

By the time I entered high school, I'd completely lost all interest in my studies. I picked fights constantly and spent more time away from campus than on it. One day, I met a guy at the mall and began flirting with him.

"Hey, my neighbor has a hot tub. You wanna come over tonight?" I asked coyly.

"Sure. I'd love to," he replied, staring me up and down with a look of lust.

Thanks to a recent surge of hormones, I'd had a huge growth spurt and now looked much older than my 14 years. It was hard to ignore the many stares from boys and men of all ages when I walked by. Deep down, I liked the attention, but I was also conflicted in my heart. Having been raised in the church, I knew that God desired people to wait until marriage to have sex. For the past few months, a battle had been raging in my mind. Many of my friends had already given up their virginity, and I didn't want to be left out. But I knew this decision could ultimately come with consequences. Was I ready to make such a big move?

I gave in to my hormones that night and slept with the guy from the mall. I betrayed my own convictions and began traveling down an uncontrollable road of unhealthy relationships, trying to fill the needs of my heart. Four days later, he fooled around with someone else very close to me. The traitorous behavior stung, leaving me bitter, angry and discouraged. I found myself wondering if romance was all just a big game.

On Wednesday nights, I showed up at the church youth group with my troublemaker friends from the bowling alley. The pastor announced to the crowd, "If you come, you stay. If you leave, you cannot come back in." He knew many of us often slipped outside to smoke a cigarette, and he didn't want us to disturb others by walking in and out. The leaders would lock the doors if we went out, making us feel unwelcome and unwanted. It was clear we didn't fit in; I was convinced our pastor had his favorites, and we were the outcasts. After the service was over, my friends and I snuck off to the bleachers out back and lit up a joint. *Who needs them?* I told myself. *These are my real friends here, anyway.*

Some nights, when I didn't feel like going home, I trudged downtown and spent the night on the Portland streets. To my surprise, the homeless kids under the bridge quickly took me in as one of their own. I envied their lifestyle in a way — carefree, with the ability to come and go as they pleased. I quickly learned that kids who'd chosen to spend five years or more on the streets were called Portland Street Kids, or PSKs. Most had street names; I called myself Nelly. I became the lookout person for the drug dealers, keeping my eye out for cops who came our way. When the rain drenched the roads, I hunkered down with my new friends on the hard concrete and settled in for sleep, while just a few miles away, a warm bed awaited me at home.

One night, my friend Kristine introduced me to meth. "You should try it. Totally different high than pot," she told me.

I'd already attempted meth once, or so I thought, but it had turned out to be nothing but Epson salt. I snorted meth with her and a guy friend that night, and it was indeed the real thing. We stayed up all night, talking and laughing. But I didn't like the way it made me feel — paranoid and on edge. I decided I'd just stick with pot and alcohol, both of which were cheap and easy to get.

Determined to get out on my own and on with my life, I attempted to take college classes to complete my high school diploma. I had no interest in football games, prom and girl drama — I wanted to grow up already. Just to be rebellious, I often snuck beer into class in disguised bottles and sipped on it as the teacher rattled on.

"What are you doing with your life, Janelle?" my father asked me one night, sighing. "I know you don't want to hear another lecture from me about what's right and wrong, but I think you know in your heart what to do. Your mom and I have been asking God to take care of you."

"Don't worry about me, Dad. I'm fine," I replied, running my hands through my short, spiked pink hair. "I'm really not a bad kid." But even as I said the words, something stung deep inside. As I lay down that night, settling for my own bed instead of under the damp Portland bridge, I thought back to when I was 7 years old. The pastor had invited those who wanted to ask Jesus into their heart to pray along with him one Sunday morning. He said Jesus had come to earth and died on a cross for the wrong things we'd done so that we would not have to spend eternity without him. By inviting him into our hearts and asking him to forgive us, we could enjoy a relationship with him forever. Though I'd heard many Bible stories by then and memorized many verses from the Bible in the Good News Bears Club and Awana kids program, I didn't fully understand what it meant to have a relationship with God.

I did know that heaven sounded like a wonderful place and that I didn't want to go to hell, so I wanted to make sure Jesus was really in my heart. After that, I'd asked him into my heart several more times, just to be sure, even though the pastor said once was enough, if we really meant it.

Nothing magical had happened at that moment — no fireworks or flash of bright light or electric shock through my toes. But I had known from that moment on that Jesus would always be there for me. He was that best friend if I needed someone to talk to, if I was afraid or discouraged or down on the world. Even if I messed up time and time again, I could still come back to him and ask for forgiveness, and he would accept me as I was. I found great comfort in that, but I also wasn't sure this whole church thing was for me right now. I was an outcast at youth group, and I knew that people looked down on me for not following the rules. Life outside the church seemed more exciting, and if I wanted to come back to all of this spiritual stuff someday, I knew it would be waiting for me where I left off.

One day in mid-October, I met the most beautiful guy I'd ever laid eyes on in my life. Justin's mother was the Campbell soup lady while I was in grade school, and my brother had classes with his siblings. A mechanic, Justin rode a motorcycle, which I found especially hot. Tall, with chiseled muscles, sparkling blue-green eyes and dirty blond hair, Justin looked like the man of my dreams. Within moments after exchanging words, I pictured myself spending the rest of my life with him, my internal lust knowing no constraints.

On November 30, 2002, I was running on the sidewalk to catch the bus when a Honda sedan sped out of a parking lot and hit me. I flew up in the air and landed under the wheel of the bus. As I lay there, reeling in pain and in shock, the bus driver rushed to my side, followed by Shannon, who had been waiting on board for me.

"Oh, my gosh, Janelle! Are you okay?" she cried, her eyes wide and panicked as she saw me crumpled in a heap on the concrete.

But I was too weak to reply. They helped me onto the bus and sped off toward the nearest hospital, Providence Portland, 10 blocks away. Shannon checked me into the emergency room. I slipped out of consciousness, and when I awoke, strange faces stared into mine.

"What happened?" I asked groggily, glancing around. I tried to move my neck but found I could not. My entire body ached, and slowly, I pieced the horrific events together in my mind.

"You were hit by a car," the doctor explained. "You've got a lot of soft tissue damage to your spine and neck, which will require extensive chiropractic treatment. But quite frankly, young lady, you're lucky you were not more seriously injured. You've got the Honda emblem bruised into the side of your leg as a reminder of the impact."

I tried to smile, but even that little movement hurt. "Wow," was all I could say.

The incident shook me, but when I recovered, I returned to the streets and continued spending time with my old crowd. A new guy caught my interest. Aaron hung out at the downtown Portland square. Though shorter and not as strikingly handsome as Justin, he intrigued me with his spiky blond hair and mysterious green eyes. I soon learned Aaron was a stripper at the gay clubs in town. Within weeks, I was sleeping with both him and Justin.

On Valentine's Day 2003, I learned I was pregnant. I sat with my friend, staring at the little plastic stick that verified the shocking news.

"What are you gonna do?" my friend asked.

I shrugged. "I'm going to have a baby, I guess." I had never believed in abortion, and a few of my friends had already had babies, so I was used to changing diapers. As I did the math, I quickly ascertained that the father was Aaron, not Justin, my dream guy.

"I have to tell you something," I told Aaron that chilly February night. "I'm pregnant."

Aaron nodded, taking in the news. I wondered if he was trying to assess how he — a stripper — could provide for a newborn. But to my surprise, he remained calm. "Everything is going to be okay," he said confidently. "It's all going to work out, Janelle."

I broke the news to my parents next. "I guess you're

going to find out sooner or later, so I might as well tell you that I'm pregnant," I said, my voice cracking.

My mother's eyes welled with tears. "Well, Janelle," she said at last, "this certainly isn't the plan we had for your life, but we support you keeping the baby, and we'll help you in any way we can."

My father nodded. "We'll figure this out," he added, but his voice held a twinge of sadness.

Though my belly grew, I continued to hang out with the crowd downtown, sell drugs and smoke pot. One day, when I was 13 weeks along, I finished smoking a joint with my friends and rolled the last of the baggies they planned to sell that day. As I climbed on the MAX train to head home, everything around me started to go black. I felt myself grow woozy and grabbed the metal rail for support. The next few moments were a blur of confusion as my entire body began to convulse.

When the train came to a halt, I managed to stumble out the doors and called my father to come pick me up. Suddenly, I felt as if I'd wet my pants. But when I looked down, I was horrified to see blood instead. Panic seized me as I sat there on the bus bench, helpless, alone and terrified. What on earth was happening to me? Had I just lost the baby?

My father picked me up and took me to the hospital. My heart raced as the ultrasound technician ran the wand over my belly. "Well, I see one healthy baby in there," she said. "It looks like you may have been carrying twins and miscarried the other one."

A RAINBOW OF PROMISE

A wave of relief washed over me. "So the baby is okay?" My mind raced to the weed I'd smoked just hours earlier. I knew it wasn't laced because none of my friends or customers who had smoked it had had any problems with it. But had it caused something to go wrong? Either way, I knew one thing — I was done using drugs. For good — or so I thought.

I was at a crossroads. I knew I should go home, get my life straightened out and focus on taking care of my body and my baby, but instead, I returned to the streets. This time, I hooked up with an infamous drug dealer named Greg. With a shaved head, goatee and a teardrop-shaped face, Greg was otherwise rather plain-looking. But I liked the power he commanded on the streets — everyone knew who he was, and everyone respected him.

One evening, after Greg left to sell his last few bags of weed, I stepped outside of my friend's downtown apartment where we'd been crashing and saw three cop cars outside. I cradled my six-months-pregnant belly protectively as six cops marched toward the building and approached me.

"You're under arrest for robbery," one cop barked, holding up a pair of handcuffs.

"Robbery?" I gasped. It was true I hung around with drug dealers, but I hadn't been stealing. Rather than protest, however, I complied as the cop threw me in the back of the patrol car and sped off.

"You like country music?" he asked, flipping through the radio stations as we drove.

I gulped. "Yeah, it's cool," I replied slowly. My heart raced. I thought back to the girl who'd stopped by the apartment earlier. I had called her to pick up her things I'd found in the closet. Was it possible she'd been the victim of the robbery?

When we arrived at the station, Greg was in a cell; he'd been arrested, too! The detectives placed me in a holding cell right next to him. A bit later, they pulled me into an interrogation room and opened up a backpack — *my* backpack.

"Recognize this?" the detective asked, staring at me.

I nodded and gasped. "Yes, it's mine," I whispered.

"We found stolen jewelry inside. Got any idea where it came from?"

I shook my head vehemently. "None. I swear."

Greg was booked for drug possession charges and remained in jail for 30 days. No charges were pressed against me. I was released to my parents 14 hours later and soon learned that the stolen goods had been planted in my backpack by one of the guys who'd come to the house. I was grateful to be found innocent but angry that I'd been set up.

"Now what?" I asked Greg. I was due in just a couple of months and had little money to my name. I knew that life on the streets was no way to raise a baby, but I wasn't ready to go home yet.

Greg and I began dating more seriously and slept in a tent in his grandmother's backyard in North Portland. Every so often, I went home to my own warm bed to get a good night's sleep. We soon got a two-bedroom apartment together.

Aaron called one day, furious at me. "What are you doing, dating that loser drug dealer?" he screamed. "You're gonna make a terrible mother! The minute that baby is born, I'm gonna take him away from you."

I hung up on him, enraged. Aaron was no superstar himself, stripping at a gay club. What right did he have calling me a horrible mother when I hadn't even had the baby yet? I wanted to be the best mom possible, even in the midst of my situation, and his words had stung me deeply.

On October 23, 2003, I went into labor and admitted myself to the hospital under a false name to protect myself and the baby from Aaron. When little Christian entered the world, a healthy 7 pounds, 11 ounces, my mother, sister and father were there to witness the birth and celebrate with me. My father cut the umbilical cord. Tears filled my eyes as I watched him cradle his new grandson in his arms. I knew my father was disappointed with many of the choices I'd made, but he'd stuck by my side through it all, a silent supporter through difficult times.

The staff administered double arm bands to me and Christian and alerted the front desk about Aaron, who was to be arrested if he set foot in the hospital during my stay. I went home with Greg, but five days later, Aaron called to see if I'd had the baby.

"I had a little boy," I told him hesitantly.

"I'd love to see him," Aaron said sweetly, his harsh

voice replaced by a softer tone. "Do you think we could arrange something?"

I agreed to meet Aaron at the local mall, where security guards were present in case he tried anything funny. To my surprise, he was pleasant and affectionate with Christian. "Let me help you out," he suggested. "I'll take care of him half the time so you can get some rest. What do you think?"

I was taken aback by his interest in the baby. But I was also exhausted and knew I didn't have the means to care for Christian full time alone. "Well, all right, I guess we can try out that arrangement," I agreed reluctantly.

A few weeks later, a year to the date after my first car accident, another Honda sideswiped me while I was driving. I was uninjured, but the incident rattled me. It seemed no matter where I went trouble seemed to follow.

Aaron quickly proved to be an unfit father. When I showed up at his house, I found Christian crawling around on the flea-infested floor, unsupervised. And once, he dropped the baby off at his sister's house, where I found her blowing smoke into Christian's face when I arrived.

"I thought you'd changed, Aaron," I cried. "But you haven't changed a bit, I see."

Furious by his lack of concern for Christian's welfare, I took him to court and obtained full custody of my son. Meanwhile, Greg and I got an apartment near my parents' house, and I continued to date him. But our relationship wasn't so great, either. Greg and I enjoyed pornography, and watching dirty videos in our bedroom became a regular routine for both of us. I knew deep down the habit was wrong, but both Greg and I were hooked and unable to be physically attentive without watching porn.

Greg began to grow very controlling. One day, after he drank too much, I found him in my bedroom, throwing my clothes around. "What are you doing?" I demanded.

He whirled around, his eyes fiery. "What the h*** are *you* doing?" he lashed out, holding up my leopard print dress. "You going out cheating on me, huh?"

"Yeah, right. Come on, Greg. Cool it. I know you're drunk," I replied, trying to keep my voice calm.

But he pulled out his lighter and lit my clothes on fire. Horrified, I watched my dress go up in flames. "Are you crazy?!" I screamed. I grabbed a pot of water and doused the fire, but it was too late — my clothes were ruined. Furious, I stormed out of the room and decided to break up with him.

My car died one day, and I called Justin to see if he could help fix it. When he showed up, I was just as enamored as ever. I watched dreamily as he tinkered with the engine, his chiseled arms peeking out from under the hood. *I bet he would make a great stepfather to Christian,* I thought to myself. I was starting to realize Greg was no good for me, but I was afraid to leave him and be alone. Perhaps if Justin came back into the picture, I could have my happily ever after.

Justin hung around for the next couple days and played with Christian, and I was impressed with his paternal skills. I was desperate for another chance for a relationship with Justin, but to my heartbreak his attention was self-absorbed, and soon he was gone again! My pain hit an all-time low.

In June 2005, I moved to Salem, an hour away, and got a job at a retirement home. I had just decided maybe I could settle down there and get away from the chaos for good when another blow came my way. While driving down a two-lane road one afternoon, a car made a left turn in front of me, causing me to T-bone the vehicle. As my car skidded across the road, my head slammed against the steering wheel, and everything began to spin in slow motion.

In a daze, I climbed out of the car and picked up my license plate off the road. Though I was shaken, it appeared all my bones were intact, and there was little blood. But within a few days, I realized my short-term memory was affected. I continuously misplaced and forgot things and often could not remember where I was going or what I was doing. Concerned that I could not care for Christian on my own, I returned to Portland so my family could help me.

I transferred to the retirement home in Portland and continued working. My brother had a coworker named Anthony who was looking for a roommate. We checked out a duplex with a basement and decided to move in together; the place was just a few blocks from my parents' house. Anthony, a slender guy with dark hair, was an avid health nut who practiced martial arts; I wasn't interested in him as more than a friend. Greg and I got in contact again, but I made no attempt to begin dating him again.

The night Anthony and I moved into our new apartment, Greg stopped by to check it out. We walked across the street to the nearby grade school and chatted for a moment. I shared with him that a guy at work had tried to sexually harass me, and he grew angry.

"You probably egged him on!" he snarled, lunging at me. He shoved me against the brick wall of the school building, and I slid down to the ground like a limp ragdoll. Just as I started to get my footing, he grabbed my neck and tried to snap it back. Then, as if I wasn't worth it, he let go, snorted in disgust and walked away.

Reeling from Greg's burst of anger, I called Anthony to come help me home. Anthony raced to my side and carried me back to our apartment. "Are you okay?" he asked, his eyes filled with horror as I explained what happened. "Why do you even let that guy come around?"

I was still shaking as he set me down on the couch. "I don't know," I mumbled, tears filling my eyes. "But I'm really done with him now."

Christian turned 2 years old 10 days later. During his party, I glanced over at Anthony several times and suddenly wondered why I hadn't realized how great he was before. That night, after I tucked Christian into bed, we began to talk.

"Janelle, why don't we get married?" he said. "I know it's fast, but it's obvious we both care for each other." He paused, searching my eyes. "Do you think it's crazy?"

I laughed. "No, I think it's perfect!" Anthony was unlike any guy I'd ever dated before. He was a virgin and wanted to remain that way until his wedding day. He was also a gentleman who had the utmost respect for me and truly cared for my son as well. He made a steady living as a professional video gamer, and I knew he could provide for our family. Anthony would make a great husband.

"Would it be even crazier if I said I didn't want to kiss until we got married?" he pressed, grinning.

I shook my head. "No, I think that sounds like a great plan." I was determined to do things right for once. My life with Anthony would be the beginning of my fresh start.

We chose to get married two months later in a small chapel at the church my parents had gotten married at years before. An intimate group of 40 people came to watch us say our vows. It was frigid outside as I slipped into my beautiful cream-colored gown. I felt like a princess as I twirled around in front of the mirror. Anthony and I had shared a whirlwind romance, but I was confident our relationship would stand the test of time, despite the skeptics who predicted otherwise.

Anthony and I opened a daycare out of our home. One day, Anthony and I talked about purchasing a used vehicle. I suggested we ask Justin to take a look at the vehicle we had purchased. Anthony thought it was a good idea, so Justin came over that evening. I watched as the two men talked shop about cars and video games. I could not get my prior relationship with Justin out of my head.

Later that year, I learned I was pregnant, and on February 11, 2007, we welcomed our son, Jonathan, into the world. I was thrilled to be a mother again; at last, the pieces of my life seemed to be falling together.

Two months after Jonathan was born, I got into another car accident when a vehicle sideswiped mine. Though I was not seriously hurt, the incident only added to my already growing list of physical ailments from the previous accidents. A year later, I decided we should close the daycare and seek another direction in life.

"What do you think about going back to school?" Anthony asked after we tucked the boys in one night. "I hear Mt. Hood Community College has some great programs. We could apply for financial aid and both enroll."

I hadn't been a huge fan of high school and had gone on to take college courses so I could graduate early. I'd wanted to go back to school, but life always seemed to get in the way. "I think it could be really good for us," I agreed after mulling it over for a bit.

We moved to Troutdale, Oregon, and settled into a little apartment in the country. The boys attended daycare on campus, while we went to class each day. I was content with our new life; my days on the streets doing drugs seemed a million years away.

But it didn't take long for trouble to brew in our home. I went out to a karaoke bar one night and discovered how much I enjoyed singing for the crowd. I began leaving the boys home with Anthony and going out more. One night,

I met a handsome guy named David. He was tall, with a sturdy build and a smooth bald head. He told me, in his drunken state, that his wife had just cheated on him.

"I'm so sorry," I told him sympathetically. "That must be really awful."

I frequented the karaoke bar several more times, not realizing that my nights out were slowly eroding the trust in my marriage. I never initiated anything romantically with anyone I met, but after I attended a benefit concert with an old friend one night, rumor spread that I had cheated on Anthony, and he grew furious.

"I swear, the guy I was sitting with at dinner was just an old friend," I promised him.

But Anthony didn't buy it. The tension grew in our home, and by the end of August 2009, we had separated. Our marriage had lasted much longer than our friends had guessed it might, but I was still saddened. I cared for Anthony and didn't want things to end as they did. After all, he was the father of my child.

Anthony moved out, and I reached out to Justin once again. I knew he had a son now, and I tried to extend an olive branch, but it backfired on me. Anthony called telling me to leave Justin alone. I had no idea they had exchanged numbers that night he came to look at our car. I was devastated, but I knew I was going to have to get over him, and I was only going to accomplish this with God's help.

After years of inappropriate relationships, a failed marriage and a shattered heart, I turned to my new friend

David. There was an undeniable chemistry between us, and it wasn't long before my old addictions took control, and we were sleeping together. It hadn't even been a month since Anthony and I had separated.

At the end of September, we took a trip to the beach and enjoyed a weekend together. "I have an idea," I told David excitedly. "Let's make a list of 'firsts,' things we've never done at the beach before."

David, always one for adventure, thought the list idea was fun. I knew David had recently gotten out of a difficult marriage himself, and I had no intention of marrying him tomorrow. I only knew that we were having a good time together right now. We were inseparable for the next couple of months. I started feeling guilty inside for dating him while still married to Anthony. My heart stirred to try to work out my marriage, and so I called it quits with David, but the damage to my marriage was overwhelming and ultimately beyond repair.

In March 2010, David and I got back together, and he moved in with me and the boys. That summer, I learned I was pregnant. I was excited about having another child, but during a routine doctor's visit, I learned some bad news.

"I'm afraid your HcG levels are dropping," the doctor said grimly. "Your body will probably expel the baby on its own in due time."

I was devastated by his words. Soon after, I experienced excruciating abdominal pain and went back to the doctor. He confirmed that I was bleeding internally because my left fallopian tube had ruptured. I rushed to the hospital in hopes of saving the baby, but the doctor there only had more disheartening news.

"This is what we call an ectopic pregnancy," she explained. "I'm afraid it's too late to save the baby, but we'll try to save your fallopian tube."

After the surgery, the doctor explained that she had to remove my entire left tube. "The possibility of conceiving again is 50/50 at best," she said grimly. "To be honest, I'm not sure if you'll ever be able to have children again."

The loss of the baby put a strain on my relationship with David. His ex-wife had a little girl, Mia, with whom he was very close, but he had always wanted children of his own. We continued to date but grieved in our own ways. When I tried to talk to him about it, he completely shut down.

"We'll try again for a baby," I promised. "It will happen, I know it will." But deep down, I wondered if the doctors were right. My body had already been through so much trauma; was there any hope left?

David and I attended church together on Sunday, but both of us felt like we were going through the motions. I felt people's eyes on us as we sat in the pews, and I wondered what they thought. Were they concerned for my welfare, interested in my future or silently condemning me for the things I had done. In my heart, I had always known right from wrong. I had never let go of my faith in Jesus; I had made some bad choices along the way, and I knew it. Everyone makes mistakes, but I hadn't reached the breaking point yet. My rock bottom was still ahead of me.

In September, David and I broke up. The pain of losing the baby took its toll on the relationship, and we started growing emotionally distant. David and I began seeing other people, but we maintained a casual relationship. I could not get him out of my head or my heart, and deep down, I hoped that one day we might be together for good.

In October, I got in yet another car accident, bringing my total to a whopping five. After being rear-ended by a car flying at a high speed, I was sore but not seriously injured. I thanked God for protecting me yet again.

In November, I moved back in my parents' house with the boys and began dating a guy named Brett from school. I told David I was done with him for good and focused on school, my boys and my new boyfriend. Brett smoked marijuana heavily and had a pornography problem. Before long, I found myself drawn back into the old lifestyle I had vowed to never touch again.

What are you doing, Janelle? I asked myself one night, feeling dirty after smoking a joint and watching a porn video with Brett. As the last of the marijuana smoke curled into the air, my mind flashed to that little girl who sat in church as a child, memorized verses in the Good News Bears Club and sang songs about Jesus on Sunday. *I'll come back to God someday,* I'd told myself. As I'd grown older, I made the conscious decision to screw up my life, to see just how far I could push things with God and the world. At times, I'd thought I'd hit rock bottom, but did I still have further to go? And would God still be waiting for me if I did hit the bottom, ready to hoist me back up and into his arms?

Later I moved out of my parents' home and into a one-bedroom apartment overlooking the beautiful coastline of the Columbia River. Anthony and I agreed to a 50/50 custody of the boys so we could equally spend time with them.

In June 2011, I graduated from Mt. Hood with two associate's degrees. Though Brett came to my graduation, it was David I wanted to share my special day with.

"Guess what? I did it! I graduated!" I told David excitedly over the phone. "I know no one thought I would amount to anything after having a kid at 18, but here I am!"

"That's awesome, Janelle. I knew you could do it," David said, his voice warm and friendly. "I want to see you again."

"I want to see you again, too," I replied softly, my heart warming at the thought. David and I reunited and began building our relationship. I tried to ignore it, but I knew deep down that there was still something missing.

I began college classes to get my bachelor's degree that summer. Later that fall, we moved back in together, and I discovered we were pregnant. Despite what the doctors had said, I'd been able to conceive!

"We're going to have a baby!" I gushed to David, wrapping my arms around his strong chest. I wondered if our child would have my blond hair and blue eyes or his chiseled features. We would soon find out!

I endured a difficult pregnancy; at one point, the entire right side of my body went numb. During a routine ultrasound, we learned we were having a boy, and we were both thrilled. My house would be filled with soccer balls, muddy shoes, baseball gloves and video games, and I would love every minute of it.

One warm May evening, I turned to David and said with a smile, "So are you ever going to marry me?"

"Yes," he replied.

"Great, I'm going to start planning the wedding," I said eagerly.

Everything was ready for our wedding on July 7, except for one thing. David had not formally proposed. Finally, on the Fourth of July, David dropped to his knees as we lit off fireworks. "Janelle, will you marry me?"

"Of course!" I cried, throwing my arms around him.

David and I were married three days later on the top of Rocky Butte in Northeast Portland. A beautiful castle sat atop the mountain, and the Columbia River stretched out like a shiny blue ribbon below. Our immediate family came to celebrate with us, and we topped off the evening with some karaoke, which seemed especially fitting considering how we had met!

David and I continued to attend church at Anthem, where I worked as the check-in person for the children's nursery. I enjoyed this position because I could act as a "bodyguard" and protect the kids at the front door. I had hesitated to get too involved in church in the past because I worried people might judge me for my past lifestyle. But as I began to put names with their smiling faces and get to know their stories, I realized that they were people just like me. Many of them had a past, but they had come to Anthem because the church represented a place where folks could come as is and know that they were still accepted and loved. We were truly thankful that this church was different, allowing us to grow at our own pace and ready to help us develop our relationship with God. Little did I know how important that would be to me in the days just ahead.

On August 8, 2012, little Joshua came into the world, pink-cheeked, chubby and perfectly beautiful. The events of my difficult delivery soon melted away when I gazed into his little eyes. David and I quickly fell into a routine, taking turns caring for the kids, while I returned to college classes and he went to work.

On October 6, I awoke at 6:30 a.m. to the blare of the alarm clock. David realized he was late for work and rushed off. I slid away from Joshua so as not to disturb him. After heading downstairs, I made some coffee, smoked a cigarette and started working on my computer. At 7:30, I glanced at the clock and wondered if I should wake Joshua up, but decided to let him sleep a bit longer. At 8:15, I went upstairs to grab my phone and check in on Joshua.

As I walked closer, I realized, to my horror, that his little chest was not rising. Immediately, I scooped him up and grabbed my phone to dial 911. I frantically ran downstairs and outside, where a construction crew was working nearby.

"My son is not breathing!" I screamed to the first worker I encountered. When I glanced down, I saw blood trickling from Joshua's nose. The 911 operator instructed me to lay him on a flat surface and administer chest compressions, and a man named Campbell arrived by my side to assist with the rescue breathing.

When the paramedics arrived, I ran inside for my shoes and called David, but he did not answer. I then called my mother and screamed, "Joshua is dead! You need to get here now!" David then returned my call, and I asked him to come home. Little Joshua wasn't breathing.

The moment I hung up, I collapsed in the gravel driveway, arms stretched toward the ambulance. I screamed and prayed, "Jesus, please be with my son! Jesus, be with my son!"

My parents arrived shortly after, followed by my brother. As I continued to repeat, "Josh is dead!" my mother tried to calm me.

"We are not going to say that," she returned firmly. "We have people praying."

"No, he's gone!" I argued with her. I wondered if he had passed away at 7:30 when I had that feeling to check on him. But I had wanted to let him sleep just a little longer …

David arrived and sped off to the hospital sitting in the front of the ambulance, while I agreed to follow behind with my mother. A woman named Jane from the Trauma Intervention Program arrived on the scene. I rushed inside to collect my things, grabbing Joshua's little blue blanket on my way out. When I stepped back outside, the cops had arrived. My father agreed to stay back and talk with them while I sped off to the hospital with my mother.

David was holding Joshua when we arrived at the hospital. Our son had a breathing tube in his mouth, but he was no longer breathing. David was told that there was no chance Joshua would recover, so he had to tell the doctors they should stop. "He died at 9:16 a.m.," David said quietly to me. I remained in a state of shock, unable to believe I'd just lost my precious baby. Jane from TIP stayed with David and I all day to walk us through each step. We were interviewed, scrutinized and found out later our house was taped off like a crime scene for detectives to investigate.

After 10 long hours in the hospital, we returned home. My mother and sister went into the house and moved all of Joshua's belongings to the nursery so that I would not have to look at them.

Our pastor performed a beautiful ceremony at the hospital the day he died, dedicating little Joshua to the Lord, and we had him cremated afterward. In preparation for the funeral, my father and I recorded ourselves singing "Thank Heaven for Little Boys" a cappella — an alternate version of the original created for girls. We played our recorded version and "Swing Low, Sweet Chariot" at the funeral, the two songs I'd sung to Joshua the day before he died. The songs were especially meaningful, as my father sang them both to me when I was a child.

Family and friends from all over Oregon and Washington flocked to our side to show their support. David and I held each other and wept for the little boy who would never grow up to play with his siblings, go to kindergarten or have his first crush. We had barely gotten to know him, and now he was gone from our lives.

The night after Joshua's death, I sat down with my boys to explain what had happened. I pulled out my Bible and read from the book of Revelation, grateful for the strength and comfort I found in its pages. "This is what heaven is going to be like," I told them, describing the beautiful streets of gold we would encounter when we met Jesus face-to-face someday. "Joshua is there now, and someday, we'll see him again. There will be no more tears or suffering, only joy."

The boys nodded solemnly, taking it all in. I knew they loved their brother deeply and would miss him terribly. Together, we would get through this tragedy, stronger, closer, cherishing each other more than we ever had. I would lean on the Bible verse Philippians 4:13, which read, "I can do all things through Christ who strengthens me" (NKJV). When I became paralyzed by grief, I would cling to this verse.

My father took three weeks off of work to be by my side. One morning, I awoke to find him at the foot of my bed. Before I could even speak, he began quietly singing "Swing Low, Sweet Chariot" in that wonderful, familiar voice he'd sung to me in since I was a child. I lay there, feeling 7 years old again, comforted by his presence, his kindness and his voice. Immediately, I thought of little Joshua, now in the arms of his heavenly father, and comfort and peace overwhelmed me. I knew there would be many difficult days ahead, but I also felt the presence of God stronger than I ever had in my life, holding me up, sustaining me, carrying me through every moment. My journey had been long. I had given in to temptations and made my own choices. I realized that the things that were of most value to me now were the things I had chosen to leave behind years ago. I had turned my back on God, but he had not turned his back on me.

ớ ớ ớ

Our friends at Anthem rallied around us, bringing meals, sending cards and offering to help in any way they could. More than ever, I was grateful for a church full of compassionate people who knew how to step in when tragedy struck.

The next few months were a blur. On December 10, we learned that Joshua had died of SIDS, a mysterious condition that claims the life of infants while they sleep. My tears flowed freely, some out of sheer pain and the fact that I ached for Joshua to be in my arms, and some because I knew he was in heaven with Jesus and would never have to endure the difficulties of this world. I knew there was a reason why we'd had two wonderful months with him on this earth, and I could only trust that God knew the rest of the story I could not see.

To help deal with her grief, my mother, always creative, made a beautiful scrapbook of Joshua's few precious months of life. I was so grateful for her gesture of love. I had become closer to my parents over the prior few years and was so thankful God had healed our relationships. They had always loved me unconditionally, no matter what I'd gone through, and that love meant more to me than they would ever know.

"How are you doing?" David asked me when he came home from work one day. David and I had been inseparable since Joshua's death. I knew tragedies often tore couples apart, but the exact opposite happened to us. I could only attribute this miracle to God working in our midst.

Tears spilled down my cheeks as he sat beside me. "I'm okay," I said softly. And to my surprise, I really was. Many of our friends said I was doing a little too well, in fact, that a breakdown would surely come later. The doctors said I was suffering post traumatic stress disorder from what I'd endured. And while I knew they were right, I also knew that God was bigger than my circumstances and that it was only because of the strength I found in him that I got through each day.

One day at church, a friend who'd lost two babies herself approached me. As she shared her condolences, she offered a few beautiful words of encouragement, too. "God sent his only son, Jesus, to earth. Though he lived a perfect life, Jesus was crucified on the cross, shedding his blood to pay for the wrongdoings of mankind. God lost his son, too, and he surely understands your pain."

Her words comforted me. Surely, God must have grieved his son, Jesus, when he died on the cross. He must be grieving along with me right now.

Friends and family asked me, "Do you ever get mad at God?" But interestingly, I never had.

I had often heard of a supernatural peace that surpassed all human understanding in the midst of tragedy. I now understood it myself. It was that very peace that I now felt in my heart, so different from the peace I had thought I would find in following my own plan.

My mind wandered again to that girl on the streets years before, the one who was convinced she could do it all on her own. *Someday, I'll come back to God,* I'd told myself as I endured one hardship after another. Yet even though I'd run from him, he never left my side. When I'd been sure I was going to die at the hands of my jealous boyfriend that terrible day, God had been there. And when I'd endured multiple accidents, God had been there, too. He had pursued me all along, protected me physically from harm and pulled me right back into his arms — the same arms that now held my precious son in heaven.

☙☙☙

"What do you think?" I asked David, stepping back for him to inspect the Web site.

"I love it," David said enthusiastically. "It's awesome!"

With the encouragement of our pastor, David and I started an organization based on God's promise to Noah in the Bible to never flood the earth again, the promise of the rainbow. We sold bumper stickers and t-shirts to help remind people of the original symbol of the rainbow and donated the funds to Samaritan's Purse to bring clean water to impoverished communities in honor of little Joshua. The organization was a tangible way I could give back to the community and also remind people that God always keeps his promises and that he never gives up on his children.

Just recently, David and I found out we are expecting again. The baby is due just eight days after Joshua's birthday. We are so grateful for another chance to bring a little life into the world and for this wonderful gift from God.

There will be more hardship to come, I am sure. I still have to deal with difficult people in my life, and sometimes I struggle with forgiveness. I know I will have good days and bad days, days when it might hurt to wake up, days when the pain might still be there when I fall sleep. But I have a husband who loves me, a supportive family, a church that cares for me and two boys I adore. Most importantly, I have an unseen, ever-present friend in Jesus. Someday, I know I will see Joshua again. Until then, I will carry his memory in my heart. And I will remember the rainbow, the promise of God's faithfulness.

BREAKING THE CYCLE
The Story of Joe
Written by Angela Prusia

Bodies blended together in frenzied dance, charged by the explicit lyrics of hip-hop rapper Ice Cube. A lone voice crooned above the music, slurred by alcohol and marijuana. Partiers paired off and headed for the bedrooms upstairs.

My older sister, age 14, made out with some gangbanger I'd seen sneak through her window the week before. Ever since Mom and Frank split up, Aliyah embraced the wild crowd. I lost track of her boyfriends and the times she ran from home.

I wondered if my younger sister, Bethany, had fallen asleep. Her father, heavily into witchcraft, convinced my mother to conceive a child for the sole purpose of sacrificing her at birth. Sickness foiled the plan, forcing my mother to the doctor's office where the pregnancy was finally documented. Years later, Bethany seemed lost.

My stomach grumbled as I wove through sweaty bodies toward the kitchen. Weekends meant Ramen noodles and peanut butter for me and my sisters, while Mom disappeared to the bars. The men she brought home made me lonely for the father I barely knew. Sometimes I fantasized that life would be better on the streets where he lived now. If only the soldier Mom once loved would fight his demons like the enemy he was trained to defeat. But that was crazy thinking. My old man didn't want me. I wasn't good enough.

I grabbed some chips and headed toward my room, only to stop cold. A burly guy held a half-empty bottle in one hand and a young girl about Bethany's age in the other. He pulled at her clothes, pawing her unconscious body. I swallowed the vomit that threatened to spew. Cold fear mixed with my revulsion.

"Aliyah!" I called out, running upstairs.

Lipstick smeared my sister's face. "What?" she demanded before she saw the terror in my eyes. "Oh, my gosh, Joe. What's wrong?"

I could only point to the horror downstairs.

Aliyah rushed past me, trailed by her boyfriend and several others. "Get out!" she yelled at the drunk who fumbled with his pants. The girl lay discarded on the couch.

"I'm going already." The guy cursed. Aliyah's boyfriend pushed him out the door.

I expected someone to call the police, but nothing happened. Instead someone turned up the music, and Snoop Dog boomed through the house.

My head throbbed. I had to disappear. I locked the door to my room and grabbed my hunting knife. Moonlight streaming through the window glinted on the jagged steel edge, calming my nerves. I never slept alone without protection. I'd seen too much in my 13 years. I couldn't trust anyone.

BREAKING THE CYCLE

❧❧❧

"Please give me your paycheck," I begged my mother many Friday nights. "I'll give you money for the bar and save the rest for rent."

"Mind your own business, Joe." She walked out of the house, and my heart sank, like always.

Hours later, my nightmare would materialize.

"I should've listened to you." Mom would come home, crying. "I lost it all."

The familiar knot of anxiety would twist inside me. *How would we pay the bills?*

My mom's addiction to alcohol consumed money for food and clothes.

At school, I envied the other kids, with their designer jeans and expensive shoes. I could never compete unless I stole what I didn't have. I began hanging out at the mall, staking out stores to target. The more I stole, the easier it got.

My sister's latest boyfriend admired my shoplifting skills and hatched a plan to steal something more valuable than clothes. Our plan was to lift jewelry from a department store. He'd play decoy; I'd go in for the kill.

"So, you're going in that door?" I rehearsed the plan, pointing to the store entrance from the safety of our seats in the food court.

Jamal nodded. "Let me get this pretty mug on camera, and they'll be watching me — not your ugly self."

Aliyah and Jamal laughed. She wrapped her arms

around him and planted numerous kisses near the hickeys on his neck.

"Enough already." I cursed and headed for my entrance. Several customers milled around the jewelry counter. The clerk helped a couple shopping for rings.

I jammed my hands inside the pockets of my warm-up suit and sauntered toward an open display of necklaces and bracelets. The sparkle caught the light, adding to my adrenaline rush. Stealing jewelry promised bigger rewards; my desire grew just thinking of the prize.

Another glance around gave me the courage to make my move. I took off my Chicago Bulls cap and scooped a handful of jewelry into the center. I folded my cap in half and held it close to my side, wondering if Jamal hammed it up for the security cameras at the other door.

Act natural. I disappeared among the racks of clothes, opting for a less direct route to the door. Twenty feet. Ten feet. I was in the clear. I pushed open the door, grinning with pride over my success.

"You're not going anywhere." A guy tackled me to the ground.

"What the ..." I fought back until I saw the security badge.

"You need to follow me." The guard snapped handcuffs on my wrists.

I cursed under my breath. My mom was going to kill me.

Upstairs, in the office, I gave the security guard my mom's number, hoping cooperation would help my case.

The guy didn't waste time reaching her. "Your son got caught stealing." His lip curled. "You need to come to the mall."

My mom's shock and disappointment hurt worse than the earful at home. In addition to probation, I had to take anger management classes and pay restitution. My mom couldn't deal with another rebellious kid, so she sent me to live with my dad's ex-girlfriend, Melanie.

That lasted three days.

"So you're calling my daughter a liar?" Melanie exploded in my face.

I shrugged. "I guess. You know the brat more than me."

Rage enflamed Melanie's face. "She told me you touched her."

I didn't bat an eye. Years of secrets and anger locked my heart. I never told anyone about that neighbor girl who touched me under the blankets while we watched movies or the stepbrother who liked to play Change Baby's Diaper with me. I repeated the actions performed on me, targeting loners and kids younger than me.

"She's just a 7-year-old girl," Melanie said, seething. "You're out of my house. I'm calling the police."

෴෴෴

Angry faces. The wail of a siren. Tears on a little girl's face.

I jolted awake, drenched in cold sweat. My eyes darted

around the locked cell. *Where was I?* Details came, playing back the nightmare that landed me in juvenile detention. I clutched the worn blanket, staring into the dark, terrified and utterly alone.

When I finally heard my mom's voice over the phone, her tears added to my panic. Aliyah grabbed the phone. "Joe? You okay?"

"Get me out of here," I urged, unaware of the gravity of my crime. Living in dysfunction had warped my understanding of right and wrong.

"I can't, fool." Aliyah cursed. "You're in deep s***!"

My voice faltered. "What's gonna happen to me?"

"Depends on whether they try you as an adult," my sister explained. "Then you're facing 20 years. Either way, you're not coming home before you're 18."

Her words knifed my soul.

❧❧❧❧

The fact that I was only 14 spared me extended jail time. I was released after a month and placed in emergency foster care while I waited for an opening at a boys' home. The single lady who took me into her home was nice enough, but I missed my mom and sisters. No one knew I carried my family's picture with me all the time or saw the tears I cried at night.

After two months, I moved three and a half hours from home. Reality was a sucker punch in the gut. I could kiss home visits goodbye.

Standing in the doorway of the boys' home, fear assaulted me. *How long would I be in this h***? What would happen to me?*

The dorms slept 20 boys in one room. A group shower looked more like the locker room at school than a bathroom at home. A guy barked out rules I barely heard. Soon enough I learned that our treatment group had to work together as a team to earn privileges, and we could only progress as fast as our slowest member. The set-up stunk.

A kid named Bobby introduced himself, and we hit it off. During free time, we spent a lot of time on the basketball court.

"Dude, let's make a deal," Bobby said soon after my arrival. "If one of us doesn't pass the lie detector tests, let's run."

We knocked knuckles. Taking the tests was part of my new routine, a reminder that I couldn't be trusted.

The next day I dressed in two layers. Wearing two sets of clothes made escape easier than packing a bag. None of the others in our group questioned us since someone was always hatching an escape plan.

"Remember our pact," Bobby mouthed when I disappeared behind closed doors for the lie detector test.

I passed; he failed.

After dinner, we made our getaway. When our group headed to group therapy, we snuck out an unlocked back door.

Freedom sounded as good as Sweet Home, Oregon,

Bobby's hometown, but we never made it past Three Sisters. The cops got suspicious of two kids walking around town near midnight. They discovered we were runaways and took us back to the group home.

I didn't waste time coming up with another plan.

This time, I escaped for a month before getting caught. The first week passed in a haze of marijuana. I ran again when someone got suspicious, sleeping outside until I managed to hitch a ride back home. My mom had moved, so I called a cousin who hid me in his room. Our gig lasted for several weeks, until my aunt found out and called the police.

I took off again, only to make it down the block. The cops took me to a correctional facility for kids ages 14 to 21. There we were separated by our crimes. By the second day, my reputation was sealed; I was in the sex crimes treatment group.

"Look, it's one of the gays," a guy harassed me in shop class. School was the only place we weren't separated by group.

I didn't want problems, so I ignored Big Mouth. Retaliation meant time at the compound, a concrete room stripped of all conveniences and privileges.

The guy wouldn't quit. "I'm talking to you, gay." He pushed me.

A teacher came to my rescue. Big Mouth got kicked out of his cottage and spent time at the compound. Me — I steered clear of troublemakers. I wanted to get out of the system as soon as possible.

BREAKING THE CYCLE

❧❧❧

As a kid, I learned to survive by stifling my disappointment and hurt. The one time my father surprised me by showing up to a baseball game, I could hardly contain my excitement. I longed to show him my skills on the field, hoping to prove my worth. But 10 minutes after arriving, the old man left. My heart sank. I only wanted one hour of his time, but he left. Obviously to him, I wasn't good enough.

My mom's alcoholism further added to my lack of confidence and self-esteem. We moved from one home to another, fueling the dysfunction and instability. One boyfriend promised my mother riches if she sold everything. Instead, the money went to the bottle, and we lived in his camper and a couple of tents. To survive, I'd long ago shut down emotionally.

Regular counseling and structure at the correctional facility finally began to crack my shell. Talking about my pain was therapeutic.

Soon after arriving, the staff announced a weekly Bible study led by some men from a local church. I'd been to church with my grandmother as a kid, so I decided to check it out. Leroy, the leader, seemed genuinely interested in us guys, and I found myself drawn back to the weekly meetings. He read passages from the Bible, and we talked about how God could help us with our problems.

When he read Psalm 66:11-12, God got my attention.

"You brought us into prison and laid burdens on our backs ... we went through fire and water, but you brought us to a place of abundance."

Could God really help me? Would he bring me through fire and water?

"You know," Leroy told us, "I don't look at you guys any different than anyone else."

Really? Shame filled me. Though it wasn't discussed, I learned my mother had suffered from sexual abuse like me. I hated the chains which gripped my family. I knew it needed to break, but I only saw my own powerlessness.

Leroy closed the night by talking to God. "Anyone want to dedicate his life to God?"

I raised my hand. Only God could help me change.

When I talked to God, something shifted inside me. I felt a strange new feeling. A calmness.

"I want to do something nice for you." Leroy held my gaze. "Is there a gift I could bring you?"

I didn't hesitate. "A nice Bible."

రావాలి

After I completed treatment, I lived at a boot camp designed to help inmates integrate into community and family life. In my four months there, I graduated from high school and passed the program with good reviews. I moved into my last foster home.

"Find a job." My new foster mom handed me a newspaper. She'd helped enough kids like me, and she wanted to equip me with success. "That's your first assignment."

Motivation landed me two jobs. If I wanted to live on my own, I had to purchase furniture and save $5,000.

Nine months later, I held the keys to my first apartment. Freedom never tasted sweeter. I felt like I could soar.

Adrenaline fueled me for most of the first day, but once my foster mom and her other foster boys left, I suddenly felt so alone. I looked out my new window completely bored. *What do I do now?*

Friends from work came over, and I got swept up in the wrong crowd. My mom moved in, and I drifted further from God. I started to drink and smoke weed regularly, reasoning that I'd missed out on the fun parties of high school due to my incarceration. Weekend parties turned into everyday parties.

Life quickly unraveled. In sober moments, I felt empty inside, so I dated several different girls; I always hoped to find the perfect relationship that would fill the void.

One night, a friend and I headed downtown after partying at my apartment. As we walked around, I blacked out. I'd been standing on one side of the transit system, only to come to consciousness and find myself on the other side moments later. My friend left, and four guys approached me. A fist pummeled my face, and I woke up in the hospital.

"Good morning," a nurse greeted me.

I groaned in response.

"You're a little scraped up." She consulted her chart. "But you're going to live."

❧❧❧

Life spiraled further.

"You need to find another apartment." The manager met me in the hallway soon after my hospital stay. "Your party days here are over."

Somehow I managed to keep my job, but I hated losing my place. Sleeping on someone else's couch wasn't quite what I had imagined for myself. Life had to hold more than floating between work and parties. At age 19, my future felt bleak.

While I bounced from place to place, my mom checked into a recovery home. "I'm getting help," she said when she called me one evening.

"That's great." I tried to sound enthused. "I hope things work out for you."

"I'm going to this church I think you'd like."

I grabbed the television remote for my friend's TV and began flipping through the channels. "Another time," I promised and hung up. *God doesn't want me anymore,* I thought. *I've made a mess of my life.*

My mom persisted, calling back a couple of weeks later. "Come to church with me. It's Mother's Day. I'd love to see you."

How could I refuse?

Inner City Ministry set my life back on course. After

the service, Mom wanted to introduce me to some of her new friends. When we walked outside, I noticed some guys my age hanging out and playing ball. I couldn't remember the last time I'd shot hoops.

"They live at Inner City Ministry," my mom explained. "It's a home for at-risk boys which the church sponsors."

She connected me with the youth pastor, and we instantly clicked.

"So what do you do, man?" he asked.

"Work, hang out, the usual." I stuck my hands in my pockets, deciding not to mention my party lifestyle.

"Where do you live?"

"With a friend." I hesitated. "I'm looking for a place."

"Oh, yeah?" His eyebrows raised. "We have some openings here," he offered. "Come hang out. Check us out. Meet the guys."

My mom looked pleased, but I didn't make any promises. "Okay, thanks. I'll get back to you."

A week later, I moved into Inner City Ministry. It beat the alternative of more nights on a couch.

Partying wasn't an option at my new home, but I didn't miss it. For the first time, I got to hang out with guys whose identity wasn't found in a beer can. Life really was more than getting drunk. And I was having more fun than ever.

I saw another path in life — one centered on living right and serving others. I wanted to learn more about the God these guys served, so I asked God to give me another chance.

The best part was working with the younger guys and watching several of them separate from drugs and gangs and leave their lives on the streets. One kid, Damian, looked up to me. Being a role model was new — I don't know who learned more, him or me. Nine years later, Damian is still living for God.

၈၈၈

I met my best friend at Inner City Ministry. Two years ago, Karmen and I got married. When the thoughts creep into my mind that I'm still not good enough, Karmen encourages me to remember God's promises. We attended a conference called Freedom Encounter at our church, Anthem, where I learned how much my past shame continued to chain me, and God brought healing. Now when doubt comes, I look to God, and he reassures me of his forgiveness and undeserved favor.

God is so good to me. I'm a father to three, and I have a good job, one I've held for 12 years. My wife and I have committed to give God the first 10 percent of our income, and God's math is amazing. Even when the budget doesn't work on paper, there's food on the table, a roof over our heads and money to pay the bills. We've gone from renting a small two-bedroom apartment to owning a four-bedroom home. Given the instability of my past, I am blown away.

Because of Jesus, I no longer have to be ashamed of my story because he wants to tell others the same message he told me: No matter where you've been or what you've done, there is nowhere God won't go to save you from yourself.

෧෧෧

"Daddy!" my 2 year old squealed recently when I returned home from work. She jumped into my arms, babbling about her day.

I listened to her, wondering what I was like at her age. *Did I long for my father to walk through the front door and scoop me into his arms?*

Many nights Olivia and I wrestle on the floor, but this night we were content to snuggle together on the couch. My wife and I exchanged a look from across the room. Working from home allows Karmen to be readily available to our kids, so she enjoys the uninterrupted time to prepare dinner, and we both treasure family mealtime.

"Love you, Daddy." Olivia wrapped her arms around my neck and stared into my face with her big, dark eyes.

I kissed the top of Olivia's small head. "I love you, too." I'm so grateful she doesn't have to worry about bills or shady characters coming in and out of our house, like I did as a kid. I would do anything to protect her and her siblings, but some days, the responsibility overwhelms me. My father still isn't involved in my life, so how do you learn to be a good dad when you've never had a role model?

Thank God for the church. My new family at Anthem

is helping me on this journey. They offer marriage and parenting classes, like *Growing Kids God's Way*, where I'm learning to become a better husband and father.

Later after supper, I tucked Olivia into bed.

"Goodnight, princess," I whispered.

Moonlight streamed through her bedroom window, illuminating her angelic face. Instead of a knife, she held a teddy bear. She is secure in our home because God broke my chains. He freed me from the vicious cycle of dysfunction and abuse which held me captive. I'm praying for the rest of my family to find the same freedom. And God is teaching me how to be a father; after all, he is the perfect role model.

CONCLUSION

Pain sucks! That's right. Too real for you? Sorry. Hey, when you are hurting, all you want is for the pain to go away, right? Somehow, some way. The stories you have just read are real, raw and true, and maybe you can totally relate. They tell the story of life in a broken world, our world, and yet they also give us a reason to have hope. I love to hear the stories of real people who were struggling or whose lives were totally broken by the circumstances of life and how an authentic moment with God changed their life forever. As I read this book, I was reminded of a story from the Bible about a woman who was a five-time loser in the "life" department. Living embarrassed by her failures and hopelessness, she comes alone to a well where Jesus has stopped to rest and get a drink of water. Jesus and this woman begin a conversation, and from the very start, she understands that this is no ordinary encounter and no ordinary individual. With every word they speak, her life indescribably is being changed. From her very core, something is coming alive again that had died long ago for her. She senses her failures and faults forgiven and a new opportunity to live again free from the shame of her past. Only God can do that for a life.

The amazing thing is that these same scenarios continue today more than 2,000 years later, as you just read in this book. People are still having authentic experiences with God that change their lives forever. Every time we see another life change, it increases our awareness that God really loves people more than anyone could imagine. He is actively seeking to reveal his life-changing goodness to more and more of his creation.

Think about this: How did you get this book? Why did someone put it into your hands? Is it possible that God set you up? That he brought it to you for a reason? Perhaps he wants to offer you hope — to shine a little light in your darkening world. Maybe it's because somewhere along your journey — no matter who you are or where you have been — your heart cried out for truth, for answers or for peace? I promise you that there is authentic, life-giving hope when you turn to Jesus Christ. He came to save us from all the hellish pain of our poor choices and offer us the joy of being forgiven. He came to give us the opportunity to experience life as it was created to be, lived not only in this life but in eternity.

You may have some honest questions. Can this kind of true transformation be possible? Are these stories really factual? Is it a true story, a real testimony or just a tall tale? That's what I thought the first time I heard people talking about experiences like these. But I can assure you, from one skeptic to another, that these people are not just blowing smoke. These really are the unplugged, true stories of their lives.

So here is the deal: If you want, come check us out, and make your own decisions. We want to invite you to very anonymously come, listen and experience Anthem. You have nothing to lose and perhaps everything to gain.

Ask us any questions you have. I promise you that if you will come, listen, see if we are "for real" and journey at your own pace with an open heart, you will experience God in an authentic way. You will meet others who are in the process of life change, dealing with hurts and scars from the past but filled with hope that tomorrow can be a better day. You will find people who are in the process of living free from condemning guilt. They are receiving forgiveness from our great God and support to press on.

Maybe you're unable to join us. Maybe you're just not ready to go public with your search for truth, but you are open to possible healthy changes in your life. If this is the case, let me give you a few things to consider:

First, real-life change occurs when you finally recognize that what you've been doing isn't working. It happens when you realize that everything you have tried to fill your life with has left you empty, alone and dissatisfied. Have you come to that place in your life?

Secondly, you have to understand that you are not alone. Every person comes to a point where he knows that something is missing from his life. That feeling is there because we are disconnected from God. He is the only one that can fill the void in our lives. We are separated from God because of our decision to turn away from him and follow our own plan. The result of those choices is pain in this life and separation from God's goodness forever.

Here's the best news: When Jesus came so many years ago, he died for us. Instead of every one of us being punished for all the terrible things we've done, Jesus took our sins upon himself and died to pay the penalty for those sins. God then raised him from the dead, so that you and I could experience forgiveness, receive a new heart and be transformed into a brand-new person on the inside! Look at what the Bible promises: "When a person becomes a Christian, he becomes a brand-new person inside. He is not the same anymore. A new life has begun" (2 Corinthians 5:17 TLB).

Why don't you give God an opportunity to transform your life and pray this prayer right now?

Father God, I am ready for a new life. My poor choices have brought me to a place of pain and emptiness. I am sorry for the pain these choices have brought you, those I love and ultimately myself. I believe that Jesus died to pay the price for my sins and that he gives me the opportunity to be forgiven and changed from the inside out. Please do that for me now! Come into my life. Forgive me, and let me sense your presence and peace. Thank you for giving me hope for a better tomorrow, and help me to know you better beginning right now. In the name of Jesus I pray. Amen.

One more thing I want to leave with you. Anthem is not about a "leader," an organization or a religious institution. We are not about the stereotypical groups of people who gather or attend a church, either. We are just a mixed bag of people from different cultures, backgrounds and educations. We are different in every way except that we all have a unique story of being transformed by an authentic experience with the one true and living God. And when we gather — wow! It is totally awesome! You really should come and check it out! We hope your story is the next one.

I'd like to meet you some Sunday ... and I hope it's soon!

Brad Makowski
Anthem Church
Portland, Oregon

We would love for you to join us at Anthem Church!

We meet Sundays at 9:45 and 11:30 a.m. and Saturday evenings at 5:17 p.m. at 1415 NE 223rd Ave, Fairview, OR 97030.

Please call us at 503.256.6050 for directions, or contact us at www.anthemfamily.org.

For more information on reaching your city with
stories from your church, please contact
Good Catch Publishing at
www.goodcatchpublishing.com

GOOD CATCH
PUBLISHING